ACCELERATED LEARNING

a user's guide

Alistair Smith,   Mark Lovatt & Derek Wise

Published by Network Educational Press Ltd
PO Box 635
Stafford
ST16 1BF

ISBN 1 855 39 150 3

Managing Editor: Janice Baiton
Design, typesetting and cover: Kerry Ingham

Printed in Great Britain
by MPG Books Ltd, Bodmin, Cornwall

CONTENTS

CONTENTS cont...

The Accelerated Learning series attempts to pull together new and innovative thinking about learning. The titles in the series offer contemporary solutions to old problems. The series is held together by the Accelerated Learning model that, in turn, is underwritten by an informed theoretical understanding.

The term 'Accelerated Learning' can be misleading. The method is not for a specific group of learners, nor for a given age range, nor for a category of perceived ability. The method is not about doing the same things faster. It is not about fast-tracking or about hothousing. It is a considered, generic approach to learning based on research drawn from disparate disciplines and tested with different age groups and different ability levels in very different circumstances. As such, it can be adapted and applied to very different challenges.

The books in the Accelerated Learning series build from the Accelerated Learning Cycle. This book attempts to provide a simplified and updated version of the cycle.

Banzai versus Kamikaze

In the Algarve region of Portugal there is a theme park called Aqualand. It is very popular with tourists and has as many as 2,000 visitors daily in the height of the summer season. Aqualand is, as its name implies, a water-based theme park. There are rides of varying degrees of challenge ranging from the leisurely and middle-aged 'Waterfall' to the near suicidal and testosterone-fuelled 'Kamikaze'. Participation in every ride is good humoured despite lengthy queues. Watching the visitors making their choices, queuing and eventually taking part in the different rides is fascinating.

Kamikaze is perhaps the most popular, then Banzai. Waterfall is strictly for the old, the lethargic and the sane. Kamikaze involves a 23-metre drop into a pool. The drop is close to vertical and you sit on a big tin tray to do it. Banzai is higher and longer and has no tray. You lie on your back and hope for the best. The refusal rate for Kamikaze is high. There are virtually no refusers for Banzai. Given that long queues are involved for each, the vast majority are adolescents and they are both very high, it is interesting why one ride instils more fear than the other.

With Kamikaze you drop into a long pool surrounded on three sides by those queuing to get their turn with the tray. Everyone is looking at you. You climb a long spiral staircase after you have recovered a tray. Because the number of trays are limited, the numbers on the stairway are limited. As you get to the top, the wind is blowing and you look out onto the whole of the park. You are on your own and everyone is watching. It takes time to get into position. You place your tray on a flat table and get on the tray. There are handles on the front of the tray for you to hold on to. You and the tray then sit there until the table slowly tips up. You are held in place by a retractable board. When you are ready you say so, and the operator flips the switch to drop the board. When the board drops, so do you and, veins bulging, you plummet down. It is at this tipping point that there are so many refusers. Not surprising perhaps? You have yet to commit, you have spent a long, slow and lonely time getting to here and you are asked to sit there facing down 23 metres of steel shaft as your body gradually tips. What makes it difficult is that your friends are no longer able to help you, there is no one else doing it alongside and you can see the drop in its entirety. Your willingness to say 'go' has become a test.

Now consider Banzai. It is higher than Kamikaze and the pool you plummet into is smaller and narrower. Few people other than your immediate family watch. You drop for longer and from higher and, at times, on a similar trajectory. However, the queue is up a wide-access stair. Groups of youngsters go together and cajole each other as they go. It is social all the way up. The wind still blows, the view spreads out in front and below you, but it is an altogether cheerier experience for being shared. As you get to the top, you look down on Kamikaze below. There are others lining up beside you to take their turn. Then, at the appropriate moment, you lie down on your own open plastic channel and wait. Eventually there is a desultory wave from the attendant and you launch yourself feet first down. No trays or retractable boards are needed. Some seconds later you realize that you are travelling far too fast to sit up and look round, indeed far too fast to do anything except wobble uncontrollably. You splash into the pool at the bottom 15 seconds later wearing what remains of your swimming costume. You then giggle uncontrollably between mouthfuls of chlorinated water as you fight off the shock.

Accelerated Learning: A User's Guide contains many references to spiral staircases, cycles of learning, challenging environments, anxiety and performance, personal commitment and memorable experiences! The authors take the view that Banzai learning is generally better for all-round performance than Kamikaze learning. This does not mean there is not a place for personal challenge, but an excessive focus on passing the test can lead to isolation. So too does a lonely and unsupported climb towards that test. Challenge is important for the authors' model of learning. After all, good learning occurs in environments characterized by high challenge and low anxiety. Good learning also involves risk but not necessarily the winner-takes-all risk of public exposure.

Good learning is not about the fastest and most expedient route. Terrifying experiences may be memorable, but often for the wrong reasons. Many refuse the Kamikaze challenge. This is partly because of social isolation – being placed in an unnatural physical situation with sceptical onlookers monitoring your every move. The authors of **Accelerated Learning: A User's Guide** believe that learning is in part a social construction: we learn from, through and around others. Providing support along the way is part of their learning model.

Many have found the Accelerated Learning approach to be of value. It has played a significant part in provoking thought about the nature of learning and teaching and what should and should not underpin classroom-based approaches in the UK. It is of course a model and, like all other models, means different things to the end user. The authors have deliberately laid bare the thinking behind the model so that readers can test the theory and evolve their own by-products. **Accelerated Learning: A User's Guide** is a valuable tool to take with you on a challenging journey. It is not a tin tray on a through and very fast route to success but more of a gentle, friendly and reassuring push to help you on your way.

Alistair Smith
Series Editor
August 2003

ACKNOWLEDGEMENTS

Special thanks to Ani and all the team at Alite for making it an exciting journey.

. . . .*Alistair Smith*

Thanks to my family, Jane for everything, and Hannah and Jacob for being such spectacular kids.

Thanks also to friends and colleagues in the teaching profession who are 'walkin' the talk' on a daily basis. I hope you find this useful.

. . . .*Mark Lovatt*

To all the staff and students of Cramlington Community High School. It's your talents, creativity, open-mindedness and willingness to try out new ideas that have made this book possible.

. . . .*Derek Wise*

$\mathbb{A}$ccelerated $\mathbb{L}$earning - the principles

How to use this book

'A good book is a lifetime of experience.'

This book has been written to provide an easily accessible summary of what Accelerated Learning methods can offer.

It is organized into five sections. Section one gives the background to the Accelerated Learning approach. Section two describes the use of the Accelerated Learning Cycle. Section three gives some advice on memory. Section four is a summary of good ideas to improve learning. Section five provides some useful resources.

There are a number of possible ways of making this, or any book, work for you.

You could

- flick through the entire book quickly, taking in section headings as you go, then read.

- scratch and sniff! Dip into the sections that look most useful and/or interesting.

- begin with the contents page – this gives an overview or Big Picture in advance and primes your learning.

- complete the questionnaire on pages 111–112.

- get your students to complete the student questionnaire on page 10.

- begin at the beginning, plough through until the end.

- try out some of the activities which accompany each section for yourself and see how your students respond.

- start with the question and answer section on pages 91–94.

- start with the keyword list provided in the index and do a keyword search throughout the book.

- try to summarize it for someone else.

- lend it to someone and get them to summarize it for you.

- put it under your pillow and sleep on it.

There has been a lot of practical experience brought together in this book and the challenge has been to pare it down to the bare minimum. We hope you enjoy our minimalism…

Learning principles underpinning this book

'I know where I'm going, I know who's going with me.'

- All meaningful learning involves risk: good teachers help learners negotiate risk.

- Anxiety paralyses performance: good teachers provide structured challenge.

- Learning is about seeking and securing connections: good teachers take lots of opportunities to make connections.

- Learning is best done through active engagement: good teachers offer choice, provide a balance of multisensory approaches and plan for difference between learners.

- Learning accelerates when the learners generate multiple meanings (that is, interpret the essential information in their own way and are given safe opportunities to express this interpretation through debate, visuals, dramatizations, case studies and so on): good teachers provide structured opportunities to reflect, ask questions, hypothesize and do so through meaningful language exchange.

- Learning needs spaced rehearsal and reflection for consolidation (remembering new information) and transfer (using new information beyond the class and exam rooms): good teachers leave space for this to occur.

- We commend a cycle for engaging learners with at least four stages.

They are

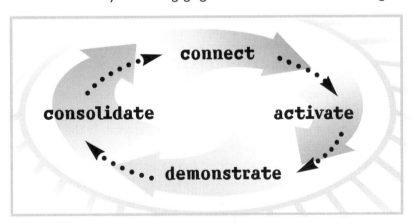

- Good teachers utilize a coherent model of learning.

- Motivation is shaped by complex variables driven by curiosity: good teachers understand the need for a variety of motivational strategies.

- The best learning is distinctive and engaging: good teachers make it memorable.

Why you should use Accelerated Learning

'A wise man proportions his belief to the evidence.'

Are you the same person you were when you attended your first ever school all those years ago? Look out some old photographs and ask yourself that question.

We would argue that this generation of schoolchildren bring a significantly different set of qualities and experiences to their learning than those of previous generations and this alone means we should constantly re-think what we teach and how.

1 Families have changed

Fifty years ago, one in twenty children were born outside a nuclear family unit. Today in the UK the figure is nearer two in five. The concept of 'the family' has changed. More combinations of 'units' are understood and are acceptable. Roles within families have also shifted. Changing patterns of employment, including more time-shifting (see 6 opposite), part-time work and portfolio working (assembling several sources of employment to make up the equivalent full-time work), has meant the end of a 'job for life' and the conventional notion of a single breadwinner. The concept of community has shifted too. Schools need to accommodate such shifts in their thinking.

2 Leisure is individualized

Leisure activities now take place in two sites – and neither is outside in the street! The first is the home and the second is the shared leisure space – the leisure centre, multiplex or mall. We now adapt our leisure to suit individual preference. In the UK, more people than ever before play soccer regularly but fewer adult males now play 11-a-side. Much of our leisure now involves vicarious participation. Most homes have a personal computer. We can watch sport on large flat screens, with a choice of camera angles, from the comfort of the sofa.

3 There are more survivors in our classrooms

More children are surviving birth. The evidence of premature babies surviving is startling. In 50 years in the UK there has been an increase of nearly 80 per cent. This comes with attendant problems of low birth weight, including learning difficulties, higher susceptibility to illness and long-term health problems. The advances in inoculation programmes also contribute to the fact that more children are surviving and more of them are in our schools.

4 We are not as healthy

The annual UK marketing spend on chocolate is £161m and the spend on marketing fruit is £5m. Children are bombarded with messages about convenience food. Serious scientific debate is considering whether junk food is addictive. Obesity among children in the UK has never been so high. One in four in their mid-teens is overweight and one in nine is obese. Doctors suggest that the subsequent health problems will eventually be more costly to the nation than smoking- or alcohol-related illness. Research shows again and again the link between improved academic performance and regular exercise.

5 We teach information migrants

The contemporary fourteen year old can multi-task beyond the dreams of previous generations. Your son can be on three floors of an internet chat room with three different personalities, listening to music he has selected, collated and downloaded, texting his friends and doing his homework at the same time! Using the prevailing technology of the age, children become foragers, surfers, novelty seekers and information migrants.

6 We have become time-shifters

The timelines within which we live our lives differ from those of previous generations. More and more we are encouraged to live 24/7 lives. In the US, cereal manufacturers are discovering that boxed cereal sales are dropping because many adults do not find the time to eat at home. In response to this, manufacturers are developing finger-friendly products that can be eaten on the move. It is suggested that in the home it is the fridge – where as many as 250 visits take place in a day – that has become the social centre. Individuals in the home operate on different time regimes but most schools shut their doors at 5 o'clock.

7 Certainties are fewer

Life in the UK has fewer certainties. The age of leaving school and finding a job for life is gone. Portfolio working will be the norm for a section of the workforce. For the rest, service and leisure industry work looms. Despite this, we are actively encouraged to create our own 'design for life' and create our own scripts. We buy into stories that support our chosen life script and the agencies in our lives pander to those stories. Reality television sells the dream that anyone can be a pop star. Research suggests that successful and happy young learners are more likely to place value in family and friends than in unreal life scripts.

8 Where are the role models?

Many children are driven to school, picked up later and no longer go as a social group with those who live in homes nearby. Which groups do they relate to and identify with? Where are the role models for maturing youngsters? Role models abound but often they promote uncertainty rather than remove it. Pop stars flirt with androgyny, sports stars look angelic but have their aggression analysed in fine detail, politicians have their family relationships and their house purchases turned into soap operas.

9 The technology is pervasive and penetrative

In my childhood it was said that hover technology would change our lives forever. It never did. This was in part because it never became pervasive. Information technologies are changing lives in a way which is unprecedented. Statistics about internet hits, text messages sent, hours spent watching any of the world's half a million television channels make compelling reading because of what they say about penetration into our lives. Each month 1.65 billion text messages are sent in the UK alone! Sources of information abound, but in the midst of this there remains a powerful need for a guide to help navigate safely through this information. This is why the educators will never become redundant. Educators teach the skills of scrutiny, the ability to discern propaganda and bias, and the capability of using the information tools in a life shaped by moral and value-driven considerations.

10 It's different out there!

The spirit of the age differs from 30 and 40 years ago when one in six families owned a car, few owned their own houses, rationing was a near memory and mass production shaped employment. This generation of children experience more autonomy, more choice, more freedoms with fewer responsibilities and yet have more tests and examinations, more physical constraints and more anxiety in their lives. Are today's children older earlier? Some anecdotal evidence supports the view that puberty begins earlier for this generation of schoolchildren. This is the generation with Ritalin at one end and Prozac at the other – a generation being 'taught' emotional intelligence in schools.

There was a time when the place of education in society, the authority of the institution and the power of the individual teacher meant that coercion was enough to guarantee student co-operation. But there never was a Golden Age!

Authoritarian control, coercion and the self-evident worth of the value of education are no longer useful tools for the classroom practitioner. The present generation of teachers have never been more challenged by the students in their care. At the same time they have never responded so professionally and with such energy.

In our UK education system the teachers work hard. Perhaps they work harder than the students. It is our hope – and our experience – that using the methods we describe as Accelerated Learning do not require you to work any harder but, given the changing demands modern students place on you, to work much smarter.

The methods described in this book work most effectively when there is a shared understanding between teacher and student as to what learning involves, what processes are used and what benefits are gained. Because we have taught something it does not mean that our students have understood it. In fact if we think they have, we may have fallen into the 'teaching is performance' trap. Learning is not a spectator sport. Knowledge is not something that our students passively absorb but something they create so that they can understand and apply. It is what the learner says and does and thinks that creates learning and not what the teacher says and does and thinks.

> 'It is what the learner says and does that creates learning and not what the teacher says and does.'

This idea is at the heart of Accelerated Learning, which engages and involves students and is done with them and by them and not simply to them. That is why they should be exhausted at the end of term and not us! After all we are accelerating 'their' learning.

Now this new emphasis on learning and the learner does not fall into the trap of downplaying the role of the teacher. In fact the role of the teacher is much broader than merely 'performing'. The teacher is introducing and organizing the learning, making it 'safe' to try, giving feedback, encouraging, probing with questions and managing the experience throughout. In this role, the teacher is the architect of learning and not the one who delivers cement, sand, water and bricks.

Accelerated Learning has created an excitement of its own in many UK schools. In this book we have tried to go beyond rhetoric and ground the model in four ways: we provide a tried and tested model, its theoretical underpinning, practical strategies and realistic solutions for teachers. You get model, theory, strategies and solutions. What we are trying to do is combine the art of teaching with the science of learning.

> 'The teacher is the architect of learning.'

We like to think that some of our work refreshes the parts other learning theory has so far failed to reach and it is for that reason that it has attracted so much general interest. In our view Accelerated Learning is not about drinking water, eating bananas, listening to Mozart and doing brain breaks. It is about a structured, thought-through and easily managed model for actively engaging learners in learning.

It is highly self-conscious – methods and outcomes are shared. It recognizes the importance of meeting the needs of the emotional curriculum at the same time as providing academic challenge. We embrace new technologies and say that they make an understanding of learning even more important for the teacher. The emerging technologies will not, in themselves, create better learners, but teachers who remain ignorant of their pervasive influence and liberating potential do so at their peril.

Creating the learning environment

'Scaffold high cognitive challenge within low performance anxiety.'

As a teacher do you...

Focus on learning?

Share the language of learning

Share the learning process

Give educative feedback

Show concern for 'improving' not 'proving' performance

Stay positive and purposeful?

Share and explore high expectations

Model the behaviours you espouse

Distribute your interest equitably

Believe that effort leads to success

Connect to the emotions?

Structure individual, pair and group-work

Provide opportunities for learners to express and explore emotions

Balance criticism with praise

Create an environment where risks can be taken

Adapt the physical space?

Work to overcome limitations of heat, light, ventilation and space

Use display to reinforce learning

Include managed physical breaks

Use movement to reinforce learning

Questions to ask yourself

'You only understand information relative to what you already understand.'

As a teacher do you...

- Focus on learning?
- Involve everyone?
- Use variety?
- Explain your intent as you go?
- Differentiate?

Questioning activities

1 Ask open-ended questions.
2 Seek descriptions, reflections and speculations.
3 Build in 'think time' then 'talk time' before asking for class responses.
4 Use visual prompts such as vocabulary linked to and organized around learning posters – a learning poster summarizes essential content.
5 Use paired shares and home and away groups.
6 Use 'thinking templates'.
7 Demonstrate answering exam questions 'live'.

As a teacher do you...

- Focus on 'improving' not 'proving'?
- Involve the learner?
- Give specific improvement comments?
- Ensure your comments can be acted on?
- Limit the amount of marking you do?

Feedback activities

1 Replace scores with improvement data.
2 Use peer marking and peer teaching in ability groups.
3 Use grades sparingly. Keep the emphasis of specific feedback for improvement. An emphasis on grades undermines other feedback systems.
4 Have learners record your comments separately for purposes of revision and review.
5 Share assessment criteria in learner-friendly language.
6 Identify incremental percentage improvements.
7 Ditch the word 'ability' – replace it with 'abilities'!
8 Abandon effort grades.

What do your students think?
Student Questionnaire

'It's what the learner says and does that creates learning
and not what the teacher says and does.'

IN OUR LEARNING...	OFTEN	SOMETIMES	NEVER
We start by reviewing what we learned last lesson and what we already know about the topic			
We agree the learning outcomes and know what processes we will use			
Our learning outcomes of the lesson are written up where we can see them throughout the lesson			
The classroom is a friendly place to be in			
We are praised more than we are criticized			
Our work is displayed so it helps our learning			
The teacher is very positive			
There is space in the classroom to do different things, for example, read, ICT, and so on			
We get up and move about			
We take an active part in discussions			
The teacher presents new information to us using pictures and diagrams			
Time goes by quickly			
We are made to think			
Our teacher uses lots of different ways to help us learn			
We work in groups			
Our teacher knows if we have understood the lesson			
We are encouraged to pose/ask questions			
We are encouraged to pose/ask questions to other students			
We get feedback on our progress during the lesson			
We get a chance to reflect on how we have learned not just on what we have learned			

Motivating learners

'All meaningful learning involves risk,
teachers help learners negotiate risk.'

Belief in ability influences ability

As a teacher you are the principal influencer in a classroom. Expectations are communicated 100 per cent of the time. Learners 'cue' their perceptions of their classroom abilities from you. Teacher belief shapes learner belief. You cannot teach positive belief but you can develop it. Here is how…

The six classroom components of self-esteem

1 **B**elonging   Learners want to feel part of the shared experience – involve them.

2 **A**spiration   Learners want to know they can improve their worth – sell the benefits.

3 **S**afety   Learners want to know they are free from intimidation and humiliation – make your classroom a safe place to be. Create a 'No-put-down' zone.

4 **I**dentity   Learners want to know they are recognized – value their individuality.

5 **C**hallenge   Learners need to be stretched – extend their comfort zone.

6 **S**uccess   Learners want the satisfaction of success – catch them improving.

How to develop self-esteem

Build from BASICS
Audit everyday practice to follow the BASICS.

Esteem the learner
Nurture positive relationships.

Provide esteeming experiences
Help learners negotiate risk.

Re-frame limiting beliefs
Make sense of experience within a positive frame.

And be clear, be coherent, be consistent, be confident!

Principles of Accelerated Learning

'Be expedient in strategy and consistent in principles.'

The Accelerated Learning model is based on the key principles summarized below. Our approach is that it is important to be flexible but that the choices we make when designing learning experiences spring from a set of well-tested principles. This allows us to be both consistent and coherent in how we operate.

We believe learning

1 is about seeking and securing connections.
Connected

2 evolves through exploration, mimicry and rehearsal.
Evolved

3 occurs when students can see the benefits of learning for themselves.
Beneficial

4 occurs when we scaffold high cognitive challenge and negotiate risk.
Negotiated

5 requires optimism about realizable learner goals.
Realizable

6 occurs through the senses.
Sensory

7 is socially constructed with language as its medium.
Constructed

8 thrives on immediate performance feedback and space for reflection.
Reflective

9 benefits from a view that intelligence is neither fixed nor inherited but complex, modifiable and multiple.
Complex

10 involves the active engagement of different memory systems.
Active

11 requires rehearsal in a variety of situations.
Rehearsed

What the principles of Accelerated Learning mean

We apply the key principles in Accelerated Learning in such a way that we:

- encourage learners to actively seek ways of connecting their learning to previous learning experiences, their present and future lives, the communities around them and their own capabilities as learners. We seek and secure examples and applications that they can relate to and derive meanings from.

- understand that exploration, mimicry and rehearsal are natural ways to learn.

- sell the benefits of learning (the 'What's In It For Me' principle).

- scaffold high cognitive challenge and share the learning processes to help learners negotiate risk.

- operate towards positive learner goals and encourage learners to share and reflect on their journey towards those goals.

- create very deliberate, carefully structured multisensory learning experiences.

- encourage lots of opportunities for structured language exchange.

- give immediate performance feedback that can be acted on there and then and provide space for reflection about content, process and transferability.

- assume a view that intelligence is neither fixed nor inherited but capable of modification and development over a lifetime.

- adopt a sophisticated model of memory systems to make the learning experience individual and distinctive.

- use sophisticated techniques for review and reflection.

We use a four-stage planning cycle to put these principles into an effective sequence.

Accelerated Learning
- the learning cycle

In Section Two you will find

The development of the Accelerated Learning Cycle

We shall not cease from our exploration and the end of all our exploring will be to arrive where we started and to know the place for the first time.'

T.S. Eliot

In this book we advocate a four-stage cycle for engaging learners and learning. Many readers will be familiar with the original 'Accelerated Learning Cycle', which was first described in Accelerated Learning in the Classroom *(Smith, 1995). The purpose of re-visiting the cycle is to point up the emphasis on learning and the learner rather than teaching and the teacher. It was always an important feature of our Accelerated Learning approach that it was engaging, active and reflective for both learner and teacher. The four-stage cycle is an affirmation of this. It is now possible to re-configure the original seven-stage Accelerated Learning Cycle into four generic 'moments', all of which link to the original and integrate into a purposeful whole.*

⚙ Models of learning

Adopting a model of learning promotes thinking about learning. We argue throughout this book about the importance of self-awareness in how learners make sense of and articulate their learning experiences. We argue that both learner and teacher make learning itself a focus of their thinking for it to endure. At the end of the day this exercise in self-awareness is not learning itself, nor is adopting one model – from among many – recognition of the complexity and messiness of learning, but sharing a model does provide a mechanism for constructing a language of learning as well as a focus for dialogue about learning.

Learning models are just that: models. They are not how people learn. They cluster around the pattern making sensibilities of humans and so are described as 'progressions', 'phases', 'constructs', 'lines', 'spirals', 'grids', 'triangles' and 'cycles'. These are all metaphors for helping us to retain the concepts and to make quick sense of them. Our Accelerated Learning Cycle is not beyond criticism and, as a consequence, is not beyond evolving into something that is 'cleaner' and more accessible. This does not mean it works any better at capturing the essence of learning. Something that is a complex, messy, individual and constructed experience cannot be reduced by this, or any other model, to one compelling metaphor. It does mean that it is easier for teacher and learner to co-construct a critique of learning and it provides a set of reference points to help. The devil is in the detail. For each stage in the cycle we provide a set of pointers or prompts to shape thinking.

A cycle is a construct and thus a way of making sense of things. Defined as a series of occurrences that repeats, we hope it can be used to promote conversations that ultimately lead learners back, through learning, to themselves. The teacher facilitates and the cycle provides the tool.

'Wisdom is meaningless until our own experience has given it
meaning ... and there is wisdom in the selection of wisdom.'
Bergen Evans

The origins of the seven-stage cycle

The original seven-stage Accelerated Learning Cycle owed a great deal to the work of those in the field of experiential learning, especially David Kolb and Kurt Lewin. It attempted to recognize the importance of environments – both emotional and physical – and so acknowledged work by Dunn and Dunn. Later, the advent of 'emotional literacy' seemed to further support our advocacy of a positive, supportive and challenging environment for learning.

Our early thinking explored concepts of brain laterality and so led us to the work of Bernice McCarthy and Ned Hermann. Bandler and Grinder from the parallel universe of NLP provided a practical rationale for structuring active engagement through VAK (visual, auditory and kinesthetic processing). Howard Gardner's promotion of a different view of intelligence and how it is measured provided a mechanism for our students to demonstrate their varieties of understandings. Popular texts on memory function and tools for improving memory helped with the detail of consolidating 'knowing'.

As we worked on the cycle we promoted the ideas of scaffolding challenge, moving to the edge of personal comfort zones and how the teacher facilitates this safely. Two very different influences played a part – Vygotsky and the idea of proximal development, and Sapolsky, a primatologist, with explanations of the true impact of stress on performance. Behind all this was the work of a loose band of eclectic thinkers from around the world, many of them members of what was then known as SALT (Society for Accelerated Learning Trainers), inspired by Lozanov, and whose work Colin Rose captured in his Accelerated Learning books for adult learners. We created a very simple seven-stage Accelerated Learning Cycle and promoted it in a series of books and workshops. We advocated sharing the seven-stage Accelerated Learning Cycle, promoting it, observing against it and using it as a template for writing schemes of work, lesson and unit plans. It took off!

'There are no short cuts to any place worth going.'
Beverley Sills

Why move to a four-stage cycle?

There are three arguments for re-visiting the cycle.

1 **Emphasis.** To point up again the learning and the learner rather than teaching and the teacher. Some of our thinking had been hijacked by those who mistakenly see the cycle as all about teacher performance and caricatured it as a set of imaginative tools. We wish to affirm again the centrality of the learner.

2 **Accessibility.** By describing the seven stages in four generic headings it becomes easier for learner and teacher to share dialogue about learning.

3 **Alignment.** We feel that many current learning initiatives and the thinking behind them can be accommodated within this four-stage cycle. For example, the cognitive acceleration approach requires cognitive dissonance, social constructivism, metacognitive reflection and transfer. We feel that these valuable components are inherent in our cycle.

✪ What are the connections?

The original seven-stage Accelerated Learning Cycle had three steps that were all about orienting the learner to learning. They were:

1 Connect
2 Big Picture
3 Describe the outcomes

We now describe these three steps as the **Connect phase**

The original seven-stage Accelerated Learning Cycle had two steps concerned with engaging the learner and involving them in sense making. They were:

4 Input
5 Activate

We now describe these two steps as the **Activate phase**

In the original seven-stage Accelerated Learning Cycle step six provided opportunities for learners to show they know.

6 Demonstrate

This remains as the **Demonstrate phase**

In the original seven-stage Accelerated Learning cycle step seven provided opportunities for learners to test their learning through meaningful review.

7 Review

We now describe this as the **Consolidate phase**

So the four-stage Accelerated Learning Cycle looks like this:

1 Connect (including Connecting the Learning, Big Picture and Outcomes)

2 Activate (including Input and Activate)

3 Demonstrate

4 Consolidate (Review)

connect

activate

demonstrate

consolidate

review

demonstrate

activate

input

outcomes

big picture

connect

A summary of the Accelerated Learning Cycle

'Make learning a focus of learning for it to endure.'

CONNECTION PHASE
Do I connect to:
- *the content?*
- *the processes?*
- *the learners themselves?*

CONSOLIDATION PHASE
Do I:
- *structure active reflection on content and process?*
- *seek transfer?*
- *review then preview?*

ACTIVATION PHASE
Do I:
- *pose problems?*
- *utilize a multisensory approach?*
- *add language to doing?*

DEMONSTRATION PHASE
Do I:
- *use educative feedback?*
- *vary groupings?*
- *offer multiple ways of demonstrating understanding?*

Connection

Make learning personal. Start by connecting to what has been learned before and what is already known. Actively involve individuals, pairs and groups. Manage the emotional climate so no individual or group feels excluded. Agree the Big Picture of content and process: 'this is what we will do, this is how we will do it'. Sell benefits. Make learning a focus of learning.

Activation

Give the necessary information to begin to solve problems posed. Use problems, case studies, role play, props, story, visual or electronic aids to help. Encourage learners to experience through seeing, hearing and doing (VAK). Immerse activities in structured language exchange. Provide opportunities for description, reflection and speculation throughout. Give learners the opportunity to construct their own meanings in a variety of group situations.

Demonstration

Provide opportunities for learners to 'show they know' through several rehearsals and in multiple modes. Allow students to share what is being learned in a variety of groupings. Provide educative feedback in or near the real experience. Place the emphasis of your feedback on improving not 'proving'. Give specific advice about process and content improvement that can be acted on straight away.

Consolidation

Reflect on what has been learned and how. Combine paired, small group or whole-class activity. Link to the process and content outcomes shared in the Connections phase. Then transfer: how could what we have learned be useful elsewhere? Preview what will come next lesson.

The Connection phase

'Start by connecting to what has gone before and what is to come.'

CONNECTION PHASE
Do I connect to:
- *the content?*
- *the processes?*
- *the learners themselves?*

CONSOLIDATION PHASE
Do I:
- structure active reflection on content and process?
- seek transfer?
- review then preview?

ACTIVATION PHASE
Do I:
- pose problems?
- utilize a multisensory approach?
- add language to doing?

DEMONSTRATION PHASE
Do I:
- use educative feedback?
- vary groupings?
- offer multiple ways of demonstrating understanding?

Connection

○————— Make learning personal.

○————— Start by connecting to what has been learned before and what is already known.

○————— Actively involve individuals, pairs and groups.

○————— Manage the emotional climate so no individual or group feels excluded.

○————— Agree the Big Picture of content and process: 'this is what we will do, this is how we will do it...'.

○————— Sell benefits.

○————— Make learning a focus of learning.

Connection phase activities

'We only understand information relative to what we already know.'

The Connection phase should help students to access and understand the links between separate learning experiences. This phase helps students to remember previous learning – what we did and why – as well as draw out what is already known about a topic. The Connection phase also helps students pose questions about the relevance of the learning: 'what would be useful to know?' This is also an important opportunity to share learning outcomes with students and to agree success criteria.

Agreeing the learning outcomes

Some teachers may prefer to connect the learning or engage the learner before agreeing the learning outcomes.

It is important to agree the learning outcomes with students. This can occur in a variety of imaginative and involving ways, some of which we list below.

When planning a lesson ask yourself beforehand, 'What will my students have learned and be able to do by the end of my lesson that they could not do before?' This is a good way of focusing on what your real learning outcomes are.

For example,

> 'By the end of this lesson we will be able to confidently discuss reasons why the Berlin Wall was built from the perspectives of both East and West'

is a clear learning outcome. Whereas

> 'Today we will study the Berlin Wall'

is not even a learning outcome but a description of what you will be doing.

Involve your students in deciding what would be good learning outcomes.

> 'Before we start this new topic, what do we already know about it? What would be good to know about it? How should we go about finding out?'

Also consider that the learning is stretching your students – relate the agreed learning outcomes to Bloom's (1956) taxonomy of 'thinking' as shown below. Encourage your students to do so as they discuss what their individual and collective learning outcomes could be.

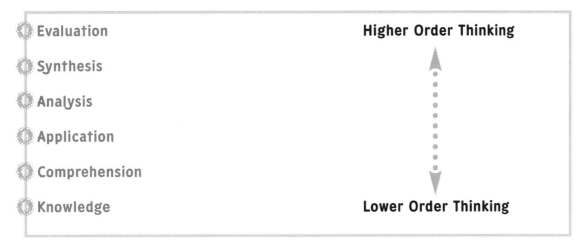

Consider the following learning outcomes

> **'By the end of this lesson we will be able to recall three examples of sedimentary rock.'**

This is clearly knowledge based and represents the lowest rung on Bloom's thinking 'ladder'.

> **'We will also be able to explain how metamorphic rock is formed.'**

This is within the next level of thinking, comprehension.

> **'We will compare and contrast the rock cycle to the water cycle.'**

This is clearly a higher order thinking skill.

As a teacher you might decide to differentiate the learning outcomes thus. Everyone will be able recall three examples of each type of rock – sedimentary, metamorphic and igneous. Most will be able to explain how metamorphic rocks are formed. Some will be able to compare and contrast the rock cycle to the water cycle.

You may wish to distinguish between learning outcomes by using the descriptors 'must', 'should', 'could'.

'Help students to access and understand the links between separate learning experiences.'

You may want all your students to be able to do all the above. Be aware of how your learning outcomes relate to thinking. Without deliberation most learning outcomes involve students simply repeating or recalling information. This is lower level thinking: knowledge.

Use a thinking wall which could be a space for displaying question prompts and where students can place answers written on sticky notes alongside or a display of Bloom's taxonomy surrounded by keywords related to thinking will help to develop a 'thinking' vocabulary with your students. Ask students to pole-bridge their level of thinking and to use the terms described on the thinking wall to help them. Pole-bridging requires the learner to articulate their thinking aloud while undertaking a learning activity and consequently helps them to better understand their thinking.

Agree what success will look like, sound like, feel like

Make clear the 'success criteria' you are looking for. Involve students in setting their own. Ask them, 'If you are really successful in this lesson, what will you be able to do, say or talk about by the end of the lesson?' Have them write their success criteria on a large sheet of flip chart paper and pin it up where it can be seen and referred to in the classroom.

In some instances you may want to pose problems without first clarifying the learning outcomes. This deliberate use of what some call 'cognitive dissonance' ought not to come as a sudden change, but be situated within the students' understanding of your purpose in facilitating real learning. So share process: 'We are going to pose a problem in order to develop a different thinking approach' is better than 'Here's the problem. What do you think?'

As a general principle, brief and debrief process and content outcomes and do so with the active involvement of the students.

Connect learning on a personal level by...

1 Break a pattern

Do something that arrests attention and challenges expectations! But be careful when you do so. A maths teacher introduced his students to rational and irrational numbers by giving each student in his class either a piece of blue card or a piece of red card.

He placed them upside down on each student's desk. On each card was written either a rational number (whole number or integer) or an irrational number (for example, the square root of 2 or a never-ending decimal). He then asked all the students with blue cards to stand at one side of the classroom and all those with red cards to stand at the other side. Unnoticed by the students all the boys had blue cards (rational numbers) and all the girls had red cards (irrational numbers).

He then went on to explain that irrational numbers were like women in that they went 'on and on and on, often without making any sense', while rational numbers were like men 'clear, concise and to the point' – you can imagine the uproar in the classroom as the girls responded that perhaps rational numbers were like men in that they were 'simple' – it was a great way to 'hook' his audience emotionally and one which his students never forgot. We must point out that he obviously did not mean any of the above and he explained to his students why he had done this at the end of the lesson!

2 Create a sense of anticipation

The French teacher dons a customs officer's cap and collects passports at her classroom door because the students are now entering France. The maths teacher starts his lesson with a mind-reading trick based on algebraic equations or the history teacher hands out propaganda leaflets to students as they enter his classroom.

3 Powerful PowerPoint

Create a scrolling PowerPoint presentation of images connected to the topic. Students are asked to view the presentation and to guess what the topic they are going to study will be about.

4 Contextualizing music

Play music as students enter the classroom. This could be music that is linked to the topic; for example, the theme to *Star Wars* at the beginning of a lesson about forces – 'may the force be with you' – or the theme to *Dad's Army* at the beginning of a history lesson looking at the home front during the Second World War.

5 Imagine

Ask students to place themselves in a situation; for example, students are asked to imagine they live in a world without electricity. They must describe in words and/or in pictures, their journey to school from the moment they wake up.

Connect to previous learning by...

6 Vocabulary search

A really easy way to get students thinking about the previous lesson that is also fun and will back up your school's literacy strategy.

Choose seven keywords from the previous lesson and jumble up the letters. Students work with a partner to unscramble the words to solve the keyword mystery. Try these:

netcnoc

het

gaelninr

7 Ranking

Working in groups, give each student a set of nine statements that relates to the previous week's learning. They have to prioritize the statements into a diamond nine – 1,2,3,2,1. This gives an opportunity for students to rank certain statements as equal second, equal third and so on. They rank against agreed criteria.

8 Early starters

Put some revision questions on the board so students entering the room can get on with them straight away. For the super-organized, prime this activity by introducing the questions at the close of the previous day or previous lesson.

9 Whiteboard snowstorm

Give students a sticky note as they enter the room. Ask them to write down the three most important things they think they learned in the last lesson – they have about three minutes to do this and can use notebooks and/or talk to a partner. After three minutes ask them to come up and stick their note on the board. Hey presto! Three minutes into the lesson and you have a 'blizzard' of pieces of paper outlining what the students think are the most important things they have learned. Summarize a number of these, making sure that you emphasize (recall is dramatically improved with review) what you think were the important points. You can now start the lesson.

10 Question wall

A question wall is a part of your display set aside for students to attach sticky note questions to. The exercise is similar to that in activity 9 but this time the students are asked to write two important questions they still have from the previous lesson. You can start your lesson by answering a number of questions and again taking the opportunity to clear up any fundamental misunderstandings.

11 '1.3.5.7'

Write down one thing remembered from last week, then swap your one thing with someone else and see if you can agree three things, now at your table agree five, and finally as a class see if we can agree seven.

12 Keywords and definitions

Put students into groups of four and give each group an envelope containing ten keywords and separate definitions on pieces of paper. The keywords can be from previous lessons or topics. Students must reach a consensus and place the correct definition next to the keywords on the desk in front of them.

Connect to learning to come by...

13 Visual cues

Provide a blank flow chart labelled with the keywords from the topic – students fill it in each lesson by adding three 'things' they have learned in each box.

Big Pictures – put up ten images that summarize key learning messages from the whole topic around the room. Ask students to visit this 'gallery' of pictures and to discuss each picture in turn.

Create a glossary of keywords in alphabetical order and ask students to add to it each lesson.

14 Mapping

Give students a memory-mapped overview of the whole topic and at each lesson get them to shade in or tick the learning outcome of that lesson.

Give students a module map (literally a map of the whole topic showing the way through from beginning to end) at the beginning of a topic.

Make a set of learning mats – a laminated A3 sheet containing keywords and images – for students to use as a desk protector; they put their exercise books on top of it while they are working but can always check where they are in the topic. They can also write on it with whiteboard markers that can be rubbed off with a cloth.

15 Artefact or prop

An activity for individuals, pairs or groups. An artefact or prop that links to today's lesson or a new topic is selected or brought in. The item is introduced and the connections are explained. Better still, ask students to guess what the prop has to do with today's lesson. At its best this strategy involves processing time before answers are generated. Bring in the artefacts the week before. 'Next week we will be discovering the significance of these items for your grandparents…' and on the table at the front you have a selection of items relating to Britain in the war years.

16 Learning to learn checklist

Students work in groups to devise a checklist of different ways of learning. Their findings are summarized on flip chart paper or on the electronic whiteboard and then collated as a class activity. The final list provides a learning to learn checklist for them to use during and at the end of a unit of work.

17 What happens next?

Get students to predict what comes next. For example, in a music lesson, the teacher plays the first part of a song then presses the pause button and asks the students to sing what comes next. Or in an English lesson, the teacher writes the first three lines of a verse of poetry on the board and deliberately leaves the fourth line blank. Students are asked to work in pairs to come up with a fourth line before the teacher reveals what the author wrote.

18 The axis of learning

A large cross is fixed to the floor with masking tape. One end of the horizontal axis represents 'knows a lot', the other represents 'knows nothing'. Students position themselves on the appropriate point. One end of the vertical axis represents 'wants to know a lot', the other represents 'wants to know nothing'. Students then position themselves according to their level of interest. Completing this activity allows the confident teacher to pose lots of questions about learning and its relevance to individuals. It also provides a review tool at the end.

19 Art gallery

Use at the beginning of a topic. The teacher has set up an 'art gallery' of A3 laminated images and/or statements about the topic to be studied; for example, particular images from the Second World War with newspaper headlines from that time; or scenes and quotes from a play to be studied. On entry, classical (art gallery) music is played and students are invited to 'stroll' in pairs around the 'gallery'. They are told that in five minutes' time they must choose an image or statement that touches a chord (makes a connection) with them and when the music stops they must go and stand next to it and be prepared to justify their decision. This provides an engaging and different start to a lesson and also has the advantage of creating a ready-made and relevant display that the teacher can refer to throughout the lesson.

The Activation phase

> 'Give the necessary information to begin to solve the problems posed.'

CONNECTION PHASE
Do I connect to:
• the content?
• the processes?
• the learners themselves?

CONSOLIDATION PHASE
Do I:
• structure active reflection on content and process?
• seek transfer?
• review then preview?

ACTIVATION PHASE
Do I:
• pose problems?
• utilize a multisensory approach?
• add language to doing?

DEMONSTRATION PHASE
Do I:
• use educative feedback?
• vary groupings?
• offer multiple ways of demonstrating understanding?

Activation

○ ——— Give the necessary information to begin to solve the problems posed.

○ ——— Use problems, case studies, role play, props, story, visual or electronic aids to help.

○ ——— Encourage learners to experience through seeing, hearing and doing (VAK).

○ ——— Immerse activities in structured language exchange.

○ ——— Provide opportunities to pause and describe, to pair/share, to reflect and to speculate

○ ——— Construct meanings in a variety of group situations (see also effective group-work section, pages 67–68).

Activation phase activities

'There is little point in giving students ready-made meaning.'
Paul Ginnis (2002)

The Activation phase should help students become familiar with the key information they need to solve a problem, hypothesize or simply remember something that is essential. ` It should be conveyed in ways that are multisensory, pose questions and engage curiosity. In the Activation phase students become directly engaged with the problem presented.

Use any combination of the following activities to activate.

1 Choose it

Include opportunities for students to make choices within your lesson – choice is a huge motivator. Recognize that students learn in different ways. For example, divide your room into a 'practical' zone and a 'research' zone and allow the students to choose the zone in which they want to learn.

In one school where Year 10 science was taught at the same time in four adjoining rooms, the teachers created four different learning zones based on Howard Gardner's multiple intelligence theory and allowed students to choose which room to work in. Surprisingly, students did not just follow their friends – especially when the reasons for setting up this learning environment were explained to them.

2 Multisensory immersion

Imagine this ...

You walk into a classroom and a large video-projected picture of a volcano erupting fills a screen. Students watch as molten magma shoots hundreds of metres into the air. Chunks of rock, some pieces the size of double-decker buses, crash from the sky.

As they watch, students pass pieces of igneous rock (granite and basalt) among themselves, feeling the weight and texture of each piece for a few moments before handing it on to the next student. In the corner of the lab a piece of sulphur is heated on a tin plate releasing a sulphurous odour into the room. The roar of the exploding volcano is almost deafening. As the short video clip comes to an end, the teacher switches on an OHP and a picture of the rock cycle appears on the whiteboard. She explains that the pieces of rock in their hands come from that volcano and invites the class to join her on a journey around the rock cycle, 'Imagine you are that piece of rock. Feel the heat as you run in molten form down the mountainside.'

This introduction to the core(!) content of the lesson is multisensory and memorable because of that. Students see, hear, feel and smell in an immersion-learning experience. This is your opportunity to create a dynamic and unforgettable experience for your students. Hook them into the lesson. The teacher might further hook students into lessons and make it relevant to them by explaining, 'the only thing between us and all that molten lava is about 50km of the Earth's crust'. Make the presentation unusual or dramatic (people remember dramatic, emotional events).

Also make your presentation reasonably short – no more than 10–15 minutes. Remember 'the enemy of learning is the talking teacher'. Ask yourself, 'If I knew nothing about this topic and had just been given this information, would moving through this activity really lead me to a deeper understanding?'

3 Uncoverage or Reveal it!

A picture related to the topic is placed on an OHP. The teacher uses two pieces of card to cover all but a small part of the picture. The students are asked what they think the picture shows. The teacher then reveals more of the picture and asks the students if they have changed their minds. This carries on as more and more of the 'whole' picture is revealed.

4 Piece it together

Cut a page of written information into sections. Put the sections into envelopes and give them out to the students. Working in pairs, the students put the sections back into the right order so that the information makes sense.

5 Label it

Take a labelled diagram from a textbook and photocopy it without the labels so that you are just left with the picture. Ask the students to discuss what they think the picture shows and to add their own labels.

6 Real-life challenge

Present the learning in the context of a real-life situation or problem to be solved. For example, '"How can we ensure that everyone on the planet has access to fresh water?" You are a team of experts brought in to advise the Australian government on a series of emergency measures for dealing with drought conditions.'

Or say to the students, 'You have been asked to prepare a lesson to teach Year 5 students the chemistry of salt. What will they need to know? How will you explain quite complex ideas in simple language?

Remember you will also need to present information in an interesting way to hold their attention.'

7 Home and away groups

Moving in and out of groups is made easier when you play home and away. Home groups are friendship groups. Away groups are teacher-directed, non-friendship groups. Just like sports teams, students expect to play home and away. For example, students start in 'home' teams to develop an action plan for a project, then move into 'expert' groups to research a topic, before returning to 'home' teams to share what they have learned.

8 Thinking prompts or templates

Use class sets of prompt sheets to develop thinking. Laminate the sheets. Differentiate them. Use them for individual and group use. Hyerle's thinking maps provide a useful selection of tools to help students to analyse information (see page 104).

9 Pole-bridging

Talk yourself through it as you do it! Bridge the left and right hemispheres of the brain by insisting that students deliberately and slowly talk themselves through an activity. Encourage them to use the related vocabulary. Isolate examples of 'good noticing' – such as when the student has gone through a practical activity such as a science experiment and labelled all the phenomena noticed. Use it for any activity that involves a physical sequence. For example, students explain a 'mind map' out loud while simultaneously tracing the connections between ideas with their fingers.

10 Roving reporter

The reporter wanders around, plastic microphone in hand, interviewing individuals or groups about their progress on the task. Every now and again the task is paused and the reporter reports back. This provides a form of review and a means of checking understanding, prompting participation and time keeping.

11 Get physical!

Get students to associate physical movement with content to develop understanding and link to memory muscle (see page 47). For example, in a German lesson, students say the phrase 'For I wake up' ('Ich wache auf') and at the same time they mime a stretching motion as if just waking up. Or in a science lesson, students say out loud 'Transpiration is about plants getting important minerals from the ground' while at the same time miming a digging motion as they dig those important minerals. In order to provoke more thought, get students to mime stages of the water cycle or perhaps their physical interpretation of the Treaty of Versailles.

12 Video conferencing

This is a useful way of exchanging relevant information between two schools or other sources. It is also a useful way of interviewing an expert or someone role-playing an expert. Set up a panel of enquiry. We all behave differently in front of a camera!

13 Electronic whiteboard

Use for:

* **stunning visuals** – use Google image search for relevant pictures.

* **turning your classroom into a cinema** using this large screen – make sure you have quality speakers attached.

* **downloading online video** – you can use Google to search for relevant 'clips'.

* **creating drag-and-drop exercises** so students can move keywords and images around to match information.

* **displaying a skeleton concept map** using 'Inspiration' software and getting students to add to it.

* **taking digital photos** of students' work in progress and displaying it on the electronic whiteboard throughout the lesson.

* **using as a 'ticker tape' facility** to flash key messages across the screen.

* **using a 'count down' clock** facility to time activities.

* **letting students use it to discuss ideas and practise presentations** – Hey teacher, let the students use the hardware!

See also section on using ICT to underpin Accelerated Learning (pages 78–81).

14 Re-creation recreation!

Provide a piece of A3 paper containing the new information the students need at the front of the class. Information is written using words and images and is preferably in colour. Students work in teams of four. Each team of four has an A3 sheet of white paper in front of them and a selection of coloured pens. Their challenge will be to re-create as accurately as possible the information in front of the teacher. Group members are numbered 1–4. The teacher calls out the number '1s', who come to the front of the class and spend one minute looking at the information. They return to the group and relate what they saw. The group 'scribe' has to put down this information on the paper in front of them. The teacher then calls up the number '2s' for one minute and so on. If group members are collaborating, they will have a 'plan' worked out to help them get all the information, for example, 'number 2 you get information from the top right-hand corner', and so on.

15 Carousel

Set up three information stations in the room. The first station has a tape recording of a spoken conversation, the second contains a TV and video, and the third contains relevant magazines and articles. Your class is split into three groups. Each group spends ten minutes at each station before moving onto the next zone. You can use a related piece of music when it is time to move on.

16 Matching

Students are given envelopes containing cut-out statements and pictures. They work in groups of four or pairs and match the statements to the pictures. You can also do this with keywords and definitions. This is visual because it contains images, auditory because students discuss their choices and kinesthetic (physical) because students are physically arranging information on the table in front of them.

17 Active concert

This is a technique from suggestopaedia – which derives from the work of Lozanov, a Bulgarian linguist who emphasizes the importance of relaxed alertness and 'state'. Prepare a script that tells of the key learning in the form of a story. Include all the essential vocabulary. Read the script aloud to the class to music. Second time around have members of the class read parts in turn.

18 Nested learning within a story

A technique that involves introducing learning points, key concepts and vocabulary indirectly. 'Hidden' within the story are all the elements the learner needs. It could be a story about the planets that does not use the word planet but instead describes an exaggerated tale about Pluto, Neptune and Mars and so on. You tell the story and then come back to it later.

The Demonstration phase

'Provide opportunities for learners to "show they know".'

CONNECTION PHASE
Do I connect to:
• the content?
• the processes?
• the learners themselves?

ACTIVATION PHASE
Do I:
• pose problems?
• utilize a multisensory approach?
• add language to doing?

CONSOLIDATION PHASE
Do I:
• structure active reflection on content and process?
• seek transfer?
• review then preview?

DEMONSTRATION PHASE
Do I:
• *use educative feedback?*
• *vary groupings?*
• *offer multiple ways of demonstrating understanding?*

Demonstration

Provide opportunities for learners to 'show they know'.

Allow several 'rehearsals' in multiple modes.

Utilize different groupings.

Provide educative feedback in or near the real experience.

Place your feedback emphasis on improving not 'proving'.

Give specific advice about process and content improvement that can be acted on straight away.

Demonstration phase activities

The Demonstration phase forms a loop with the Activation phase. In the Demonstration phase students are given opportunities to generate products that demonstrate their understanding. They can also convey their understanding through written or spoken exchanges. With feedback from the teacher or the others in the class, the learner's thinking can be fine-tuned. The Demonstration phase is highly interactive, rich in opportunities for educative feedback and student centred. Use any combination of the following activities to demonstrate.

1 Explain it to someone else

Real understanding involves 'transfer' of knowledge to a different context. Having taught what you thought was the best lesson of your life, you discover the importance of 'show you know'.

The lesson is on particles of matter to a very able class and you take students through a sequence of animated images showing exactly what happens to the particles in ice as the ice cube melts to become water and then boils to become steam. You combine this with the states of matter 'body bop' in which students move their hands to simulate the movement of particles in a solid, liquid and gas. You then ask the class to imagine they were a particle in a lump of wax and to describe what happens as the wax is gently heated – one girl stares hard at her book for a couple of minutes before saying 'I can't do this.' When you ask her why she replies, 'Because now you want to know about wax when you've only taught us about water.'

Learners have difficulty in transferring understanding and applying it to slightly different contexts. Without the 'Demonstration' part of the cycle this does not get exposed. When thinking of activities to allow students to show what they have learned, it is probably worth remembering the old saying attributed to Albert Einstein, 'You haven't really understood it unless you can explain it to someone else.' So get your students to 'explain' their new understanding to each other.

2 Hot seating

A student acting as the 'expert' sits in the hot seat. Try being: a prime number, a beam of light, King Harold, a First World War poet, the designer of the pop-up toaster, a mobile phone or a soap bubble! The student answers the questions in role.

3 Web page

Real or intended. The student or students design a web page with all the appropriate features to share their learning. Use an A3 paper template to promote discussion about editing, navigation, use of text and image. Older and more able students can do the real thing. (See tips on producing web pages in ICT section, pages 83–84.)

4 Press conference

Each group takes a turn at presenting findings through a simulated press conference. The 'press pack' ask questions and take notes in order to rush a front page scoop out ahead of the competition.

5 Walk through

A walk through is where you literally walk through the stages in a process. For example, you might label areas of your classroom as parts of the respiratory system and, pretending to be blood cells, you walk through the 'heart' where you are pumped into the 'lungs' to become oxygenated and then back into the heart to be pumped around the body to the cells where oxygen (red cards) is exchanged for carbon dioxide (blue cards) and so on. The students explain what is happening at each stage or a single student acts as a narrator.

6 Tableau

A group of students take a scene from a book, play or moment in history and freeze into positions designed to convey a sense of what is going on. They literally create a frozen three-dimensional tableau. Other students can walk around the tableau and may unfreeze certain figures in it by tapping them on the shoulder. They can question the unfrozen figure, who must stay in the role, and then freeze them back into the tableau with another tap to the shoulder.

7 Freeze-frame

A freeze-frame involves a walk through that is deliberately stopped. Use freeze-frame to pause what students are doing then ask questions (or get other students to ask questions): Who is doing what? Why? What happens next? And so on.

8 Mini presentations

It does what it says on the tin! A group of students make a short presentation to another group of students who are allowed to ask questions. The 'audience' group of students must give the 'presenting' group feedback on how they might improve their presentation. Feedback is best if students are asked to comment only on specific aspects of the presentation; for example, clarity of explanation, use of diagrams, and so on.

9 PowerPoint (powerful piece of must-have software)

Students create their own 'PowerPoint presentation' to show what they have learned to the rest of the class. They can even create a revision PowerPoint that summarizes the main learning within a topic. This can be used as a resource by other students.

10 Role play

Students physically role play their understanding. They act out stages of the rain cycle, the stages of solving a maths problem or the sequence of movements for lay-up in basketball. Include a narrator if this will make it easier.

11 Puppet show

This may seem a little childish but even older students really enjoy it. Students use card and straws to make their own puppets and props and labelled background. They then crouch behind a desk and perform to another group their understanding of, for example, the evidence for the existence of God, French fashion (in French), the Cold War or the water cycle. Talking thoughts out aloud is also a good pole-bridging activity.

12 Storyboard or strip cartoon

Create a storyboard or strip cartoon to explain a process; for example, steps in an experiment or scenes from a book.

13 Group presentation

As previously mentioned, Einstein said that you only understand something if you can explain it to somebody else. So get one group to present what they have learned to another group who offer feedback and suggestions for improvement. (See also Assessment for Learning section, pages 58–60.)

14 Pop sox, vox pops

These are quirky little radio interviews on a variety of issues complete with sound effects and musical jingles. Give the students a cassette recorder and ask them to prepare a two-minute radio 'short', presenting the most important aspects of what they have just learned. You can build these up into a resource and use them in other lessons.

15 Bazaars

Tell students that the intention is to transform the classroom into a mini-market of knowledge and information. They are to set up their 'stalls' around the classroom but they will be displaying and selling their 'new' understanding. Two of the group will 'manage' the information stall, while the other two have the opportunity to visit the other stalls to see what they can bring back. After ten minutes they can swap places.

16 Beat the examiner

Get students to create tests for each other. They must come up with the questions they think an examiner might ask and must also prepare the solutions. They then swap and try to complete each others' 'Beat the Examiner' tests. Return tests to the 'Examiner' for marking and feedback.

17 Bullet point summary

Students must prepare a bullet point summary of the key learning points in the lesson. This must be in the form of an 'essential' guide that they offer as a learning resource for other students to use.

18 Artist's easel

Students are given a sheet of paper containing a couple of paragraphs of information on the topic they are studying. On the same sheet of paper there is also a blank box in the shape of an artist's easel. They must do the following in sequence.

Step one Work on their own (intrapersonal activity) to draw images, pictures, diagrams, stick figures and so on on the blank artist's easel that will remind them of the important information contained in the paragraphs. The idea is that they make their own 'sense' of the text-based information by constructing a visual interpretation.

Step two They then pair/share with a partner explaining their images and what they mean to each other (interpersonal activity).

Step three Next they could use the same information but this time, again working on their own, select what they think are the seven most important keywords – they must be prepared to justify their choice (linguistic intelligence).

Step four Place the seven keywords in order of importance – most important at the top, least important at the bottom. Once again they must be prepared to justify their choice of order of the keywords. Because students are sequencing or ordering information, they are working in the mathematical/logical intelligence.

Step five Once again they can pair/share with a friend, comparing their words and the order of importance they have put them in and justifying their decisions.

Step six Finally, working with a friend, they must come up with a mime or physical action for each keyword that they are prepared to perform in front of a small group of other students in the class. The other students should be able to guess from the physical mime or movement which keyword they are 'performing'. This means students are working in the kinesthetic or physical intelligence.

This activity can be easily differentiated since the paragraphs the students start from can be as simple or as complex as you decide.

The Consolidation phase

'Reflect on the what and how of our learning.'

CONNECTION PHASE
Do I connect to:
• the content?
• the processes?
• the learners themselves?

CONSOLIDATION PHASE
Do I:
• *structure active reflection on content and process?*
• *seek transfer?*
• *review then preview?*

ACTIVATION PHASE
Do I:
• pose problems?
• utilize a multisensory approach?
• add language to doing?

DEMONSTRATION PHASE
Do I:
• use educative feedback?
• vary groupings?
• offer multiple ways of demonstrating understanding?

Consolidation

○——————— Reflect on what has been learned and how.

○——————— Use combinations of paired, small group or whole-class activity.

○——————— Link to the process and outcomes agreed in the Connections phase.

○——————— Then transfer: How could what we have learned be useful elsewhere? What would we do differently next time?

○——————— Preview what will come next lesson.

Consolidation phase activities

'Learning without reviewing is like trying to fill the bath without putting the plug in.'
Mike Hughes (1999)

The Consolidation phase provides an opportunity to reflect on what has been learned and how. In the Consolidation phase students focus on the content (what do we now know and understand that we did not before?) and the process (how have we learned and how can we apply our learning methods elsewhere?).

In the Consolidation phase students also get an opportunity to see the relevance of their learning to their own lives. The teacher draws out examples of how the new learning can be applied in the world beyond the classroom. Finally, in the Consolidation phase the teacher previews the learning to come.

Use any combination of the following activities to consolidate.

1 'An uplifting experience'

You are in a lift with two others and going up ten floors. It takes **90** seconds to travel ten floors. One of you will describe what you have done, another will reflect on how you did it and why, and the final person will speculate about how the learning might be useful outside of school. Then change roles.

2 Each one teach one

In pairs, what three things that are really important have you learned today? What three processes have you used that have helped your learning? When you have agreed your conclusions, share them with another pair – perhaps this time trying to agree to five.

3 Visitor from an alien planet

You have to teach a visitor from an alien planet what you have learned about a topic. List one benefit, three facts and five words they need to know about and then in a pair practise teaching your list.

4 Pop tests

Regular review through use of short but frequent pop tests. There are four types of test: test yourself, test your partner, test the teacher and teacher test the class. Of these, the most useful is self-test. Encourage varied but frequent testing of short duration. Research evidence shows that spaced, active testing significantly improves recall.

5 Team maps

In groups of four, students construct a version of a memory map that is on the front desk. Each student comes up twice to the desk so that there are a total of eight visits. The students agree a strategy beforehand but are only allowed ten seconds each time to look at the map. They can then refine their strategy before the final visit. They construct their map and then discuss strategies. This brings out issues such as hierarchies, categories, large and fine detail, connections and prompts.

6 Review poems

Use narrative verse or even a haiku to summarize some key learning. Individuals or groups read their learning poems to the class aloud.

7 Module map

Students fill in and complete over time a map of the module they are studying that shows the main concepts or ideas they need to understand. They can mark each one to show their level of understanding; for example,

red = need to look at this again,
orange = I partially understand this, and
green = I completely understand this.

Using this colour scheme creates a 'traffic lights' review.

8 Game show quiz

Who Wants to be a Millionaire with generous cash prizes! Pictionary, whiteboard Scrabble and the Strongest Link are all favourites.

9 Video journal

Recorded on video are learning point summaries. The class is divided into four and given a different area to focus on. When they review, they do so to camera. The recording becomes a resource for future reference.

10 The question box

Unanswered questions are written on paper folded up and put in the box. They can then be answered directly or handed out to groups for further work.

11 Interpretations

Different groups summarize the learning but from the point of view of different historical characters. This could include an Egyptian construction worker from the time of the pyramids; a modern-day fire-fighter; a writer of children's stories; a football manager; a nursery nurse; a tabloid journalist. Versions are compared and discussions about interpretations and bias follow. Alternatively, summarize the lesson in the style of a soap opera or 'fly on the wall' documentary.

12 Review races

Divide the class into three teams. Give each team a different coloured marker pen, that is, green team, red team, blue team. Three flip chart-size pieces of paper are attached to the board with Blu-tack. One person in each team starts with the pen and goes to the board. They write one thing they have learned on their team's piece of paper. They return and pass the pen to the next member of their team. The rule is you can only move when you have been passed the marker pen. This person then goes up and writes something different they have learned and so on – the winning team is the one with the most number of new things learned.

13 3,2,1 block review

This consists of:
one thing I already know,
two questions I still want to ask,
the three most important things I have learned.

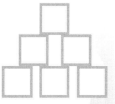

14 Passive concert

A technique derived from suggestopaedia. Using a piece of music with no lyrics and a steady 50–60 beats per minute, go over the key learning from a topic. Allow the students to listen to the music and have your voice just below its volume. Take your time, breathe steadily and use open-ended questions and non-directive language.

15 Make it into a song

Take key information and set it to a popular tune. Try this one about the rock cycle set to the tune of 'Frère Jacques'.

Verse 1

Metamorphic, Metamorphic,
Marble slate, Marble slate
Sedimentary's limestone, Sedimentary's limestone
Mudstone, shale, Mudstone, shale

Verse 2

Lava cooling, lava cooling
Igneous, Igneous
Underground is granite, Underground is granite
Basalt on top, Basalt on top.

K. Brechin

16 Circle time debrief

Rearrange furniture so students are sitting in a circle. Debrief the lesson through the use of open-ended questions designed to unpick both the content of the lesson and the learning processes.
For example:

 How do we know we have been successful?

 What worked well this lesson?

 What might we do differently next time?

Remember to allow 'think' time and be prepared for students to get used to circle time, especially in secondary schools.

17 Photographic evidence

Take photographs of students at work and display on an electronic whiteboard at the end of the lesson. This is a very powerful way of exploring process with the students. For example, 'Look at this group working together – how can we tell they are collaborating really effectively as a team?' Print photos and put them on display next lesson to connect the learning and to help build a 'community' of learners.

section **THREE**

Accelerated Learning
– making it memorable

learning
models

In Section Three you will find

 memory and learning

 memory models

Memory and learning

'Memory can be improved, though not perfected.'

Imagine if you had a perfect memory – your life would be hell! Memory is effective and healthy when we can leave what we deem to be irrelevant behind.

A 'good' memory is necessary to perform well in the public examinations through which we currently judge students' learning. Indeed some argue that the GCSE as it currently stands is predominantly a memory test. We can improve our own memory function through practising memory techniques. We can improve student recall of learning experience by understanding how memory works and adapting our classroom practices accordingly. Here are some guidelines, derived from an understanding of memory function, on how to make classroom learning more 'memorable'.

1	Use the three memory systems.
2	Prime through context.
3	Connect and chunk up and down.
4	Give significance to beginnings and endings.
5	Expect variance.
6	Distribute tests to improve recall.
7	Use places, faces and spaces.

Here are the same guidelines with some examples of what it might mean for a teacher.

1 Use the three memory systems

Researchers have identified different memory systems. When teachers operate across the 'systems' they increase opportunities for recall.

Semantic memory involves facts, figures and data. This memory system is highly vulnerable to loss, to misinterpretation and to bias. The rote repetition of facts, figures or information is unlikely to create enduring recall but doing so in combination with a vivid or unusual context and perhaps a combination of physical movements might have a more lasting effect. A list of key events from the twentieth century learned by rote is less likely to endure than if rehearsed through individual members of the class adopting a mime that captures that event, forming a sequential line and acting it out in order. The latter takes time but the pay-off is that it sticks.

Episodic memory involves moments, events and contexts. Once again, episodes are susceptible to false memory, to misinterpretation and to bias. For the teacher, knowing that unusual contexts, distinctive physical locations, experiences with a high emotional resonance all shape and add to recall allows the teacher to position distinctive episodes strategically. You learn about the fertilization of an egg, not by reading the notes but by physically standing up and creating a human model of the sequence and it gets remembered.

Procedural memory involves sequences and what is also known as muscle memory. If you play golf, you will know that your body does not always follow your mind! By practising a swing badly again and again it becomes part of motor or muscle memory. Your body aligns itself according to this learned imprint and to start again is increasingly difficult. That's why some golfers, despite years of experience, reach a limit. Their swing has been learned to such a degree it's virtually impossible to break it back down again to correct the faults. If the movement is imprinted in the muscle, it resists forgetting. If you teach with a series of complementary movements, you dramatically increase the chances of remembering. You teach the numbers 1–20 in French with an accompanying physical gesture for each number and it is more likely to be retained.

2 Prime through context

You may have had the experience of remembering an event by prompting yourself or being prompted about the circumstances in which it occurred. The UK police are trained to a high degree in questioning strategies that elicit information by defining the circumstances around which an event occurred. When your students take notes, a space for a running commentary will help prime recall. Have your older students learn how to record context and content in workbooks. The emotional quality of an experience also shapes recall. Too much emotion and it is difficult to forget, too little and it does not hit the radar. When you review key information, try to do so in a way that provides a vivid context and an emotional resonance. The example of the key events from the twentieth century (see semantic memory above) works because it is individually involving, highly unusual and thus unique.

3 Connect and chunk up and down

Humans retain information better when they can connect it to something familiar and when it comes in bite-size chunks. When you give information, do so in the smallest permissible number of units – 'five features of a glaciated valley' – and with a number attached. When you review, chunk up by starting small and growing big – one thing from last week, now with your partner swap and agree on three things from last week, now at your table discuss and agree on five things from last week. For recall, the fewer chunks of information the better – five causes of the First World War, three reasons for Hamlet's indecision – as long lists are difficult to access. A memory map is a particularly good mechanism for connecting and chunking.

4 Give significance to beginnings and endings

Watch the national television news in the early evening. They preview at the beginning, review and preview halfway through, and review finally at the end. Humans attend to what they perceive to be the beginning and the ending of an experience differently. In learning have positive, directing beginnings and conclusive endings. Have lots of little review opportunities – 'explain what I've just said to your neighbour' – throughout the learning experience.

5 Expect variance

Put two people in the same room and ask them to watch an excerpt from a film. Five minutes after the film has ended ask them what it was about. Five weeks later do the same thing. Five months later repeat the process. Not only will you get a difference between the two individuals' perceptions but also, over time, there will be a difference in how the individual remembers. Memory is more about reconstitution than recall. What we remember varies by individual and will distort over time. Space your subject reviews to keep content recall high. Actively involve students in reviewing with each other. Have them explain memory maps to each other, swap notes and interrogate each other on their own notes.

6 Distribute tests to improve recall

The one strategy that, more than any other, will help a learner recall information needed for an exam is self-test. Yet most students run in fear of self-test. Teach learners how to test themselves and each other and encourage them to do so. For example, hiding a page and trying to remember what is on it. Test informally, frequently and with variety. Make sure that you debrief both the emotional and the academic dimensions of test experience. This helps students who believe it is only they who have an erratic memory in test situations to understand the anxiety dimension of tests.

7 Use places, faces and spaces

We naturally remember locations, faces and physical position. We are good at doing so and would not have survived as a species if we had not been. Use lots of places, faces and spaces in classroom examples. When you use learning posters make their content, their appearance and their spatial position part of the learning. 'What does it tell us?' 'Can you remember what it looked like?' 'Where was it and why?'

Memory models

'The best memory techniques involve multiple systems.'

Outlined below are some simple mnemonics around memory techniques. The first – IFR – derives from early Greek writings and reminds us that, should we wish to improve memory performance, it requires a conscious decision to do so. The second – SPECS – provides you and your students with the five simplest memory tools.

Commit to IFR

Intent
You have to want to remember it. A purpose and a personal value is important.

File
You need multiple systems – such as any combination of the five described below – for effective remembering.

Rehearse
You need to go over it a few times; a little and often is best. Spaced testing also helps.

Use your memory SPECS

See it
We are very good at visual and spatial recall.

Personalize it
We remember information of a personal nature.

Exaggerate it
Unusual, out of place or distinctive gets remembered.

Connect it
Link to other known information for ready associations.

Share it
Summarize or teach it to others.

Let's take an example. We are going to learn about mean, median and mode in maths. To help we are going to construct a living graph using students from six different year groups. We have made a prior arrangement that four students – two boys and two girls – from each will be temporarily released from lessons to help. At first we organize the students to stand together in a long line in order of shoe size and note who is where. Then we organize them along a horizontal axis. They have to stand against the shoe size that matches them. We note that there are one size 2, two size 3, three size 4, three size 6, six size 7, four size 8, three size 9 and two size 10. Lots of questions are generated about sample size and about the difference between boys and girls and so on. We then construct a visual reminder of the shape of the graph using a large rope. With two curtain cords we can subdivide the graph to represent its various features.

In this example:

 students see what is going on

 it is personalized and actively involving

 it is exaggerated because graphs do not usually involve humans

 it is connected because it provokes questions and comparisons

 because they will have to explain it to others and perhaps position themselves on the graph to illustrate mean, median and mode or to talk about sample size, it is also shared.

Accelerated Learning
– advice and guidance

In Section Four you will find advice and guidance on

Homework

'People who work sitting down get paid more than people who work standing up.'
Ogden Nash

The setting of homework causes controversy and, for some teachers and students alike, no small amount of heartache. Why do we do it?

Some researchers argue that homework 'disrupts families, overburdens children and limits learning'. Others suggest that time spent on homework can be correlated to achievement at secondary level, particularly among older students. A-level students who spent seven or more hours per week on subject homework achieved, on average, a third of a grade higher than those of a similar ability and gender who spent less than two hours a week. The evidence on homework and achievement for primary age students is slim. The two camps of For and Against line up their arguments as below.

The For camp argue that:

* findings consistently show that at secondary level time spent on homework correlates to improved grades.

* homework is a link to parents and encourages parental involvement.

* 90 per cent of UK primary schools have homework policies and strategies in place.

* it helps learners develop independent and learning to learn skills.

* inspection evidence shows parents are generally in favour of setting homework even though they have concerns about the amount of time it takes.

* parents become involved in three ways – encouraging it to be done, removing distractions so it can be done and, with younger children, direct assistance.

* it can be shown that students who spend more time on homework have more positive attitudes to school – however, social, class and gender variables have yet to be properly factored into this work.

* the best type of help encourages self-reliance without 'making it harder'.

The Against camp argue that:

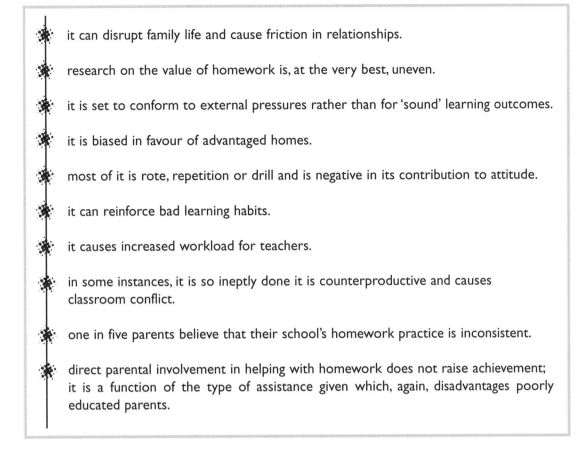

* it can disrupt family life and cause friction in relationships.

* research on the value of homework is, at the very best, uneven.

* it is set to conform to external pressures rather than for 'sound' learning outcomes.

* it is biased in favour of advantaged homes.

* most of it is rote, repetition or drill and is negative in its contribution to attitude.

* it can reinforce bad learning habits.

* it causes increased workload for teachers.

* in some instances, it is so ineptly done it is counterproductive and causes classroom conflict.

* one in five parents believe that their school's homework practice is inconsistent.

* direct parental involvement in helping with homework does not raise achievement; it is a function of the type of assistance given which, again, disadvantages poorly educated parents.

Is there a solution? Imaginative solutions such as homework clubs, drop-in study centres and designated spaces in public libraries have all been trialled with some success. Providing a safe, regulated, warm and inviting space seems to lure in a wider community of learners for after-school sessions. Voluntary sessions often have a seductive power of their own and many schools indicate surprise at how readily 'difficult' students get involved.

In schools where homework is planned by a team well in advance and is seen as an integral part of extending the lesson, the situation is known to be better. Some schools have banned certain types of homework – copying, colouring, finishing off, doing ten more – and with some success. Such schools actively promote extending or thinking homeworks. Others plan in advance that given units will not be taught in class but tutored and, as such, are homework units with supported self-study resources. Teachers using this approach need to plan well in advance but benefit from freed up teaching time.

Purposeful homeworks

1 Choice

Allow students some choice of how they may wish to present their homework; for example, concept map, flow chart, diagram, cartoon, poem, book review, and so on. This will appeal to different learning styles.

53

2 Transform (good for reinforcement)

For example, text into a mind map, concept map, storyboard, graph or a flow diagram, mind map, chart graph into text.

3 Reduce

For example, reduce the lesson to three key points and be prepared to justify your choice or who is the key character/scene/cause and why you rejected the other possibilities.

4 Prepare

For example, prepare a booklet of self-contained homework assignments in relation to the unit being studied. Incorporate a number of 'milestone' lessons to check on progress.

5 Cut up

For example, cut up old textbooks and place the exercises from them on cards or download from a website and protect the homework cards with laminate.

6 Decision making

Give students an envelope containing statements and ideas and ask students to distinguish between them and place in rank order according to criteria; for example, why did America lose the war in Vietnam?

7 Quiz

Ask students to prepare questions on the topic to use in the next lesson linking the format to a popular quiz game, for example, *Who Wants to be a Millionaire*, where questions will range from the very easy (£1.00) to very hard (£500,000; £1 million).

8 Model answers

Give students the opportunity to mark a model answer.

9 Ranking

Rank pieces of work according to well understood and previously discussed assessment criteria.

10 Mistakes

There is nothing more popular than spotting the deliberate mistakes in a diagram or piece of text.

11 Pyramid or 3-2-1 block review

These or other review techniques can be a useful homework and picked up the next lesson in the 'connect the learning' part.

HOMEWORK

Using exercise books and files

How about making exercise books and files more interactive and allowing students to record information in a way that aligns with the learning cycle?

Interactive student notebooks reach students with a wide range of learning styles, allow for a unique personal response and give students the freedom and creativity to express themselves in a variety of ways; for example, Venn diagrams to show relationships, cartoons, mind maps.

Here is how it can work. The notebook/exercise book is divided into left and right.

Left Side	Right Side
Students process new ideas	**Teacher input**
Work out an understanding of new material in a personal way; for example, use illustrations, diagrams, poetry, colour, graphics, concept map	Class notes
	'Must know' information
Students encouraged to express their opinions and record their feelings/reactions	
	Handouts
Students can pose themselves 'key questions'	
Students can review/preview	Discussion notes
Students can explore new ideas	
STUDENT OWNS!	**TEACHER OWNS!**

This system positively encourages students to become engaged in learning and to actively process information.

They are doing something with the new ideas, often using their preferred learning style, and really enjoying being given the opportunity to express their own opinions about what they are learning.

It does not have to be boring for the teacher either! Imitation and mimicry is one of the most important ways we learn, so model how to think and organize information for your right-hand side of the notebook.

Another example more finely tuned to the learning cycle works as below.

An exercise book or file can be divided into sections that reflect the various elements of the cycle with, for example, a CONNECT SECTION and a REVIEWING OUR LEARNING SECTION. The centre section of the book or file can be kept for recording information and for learning activities.

For example: Using a humanities unit 'Conflict and Co-operation'

1 Connect section

In the first lesson students are given the key questions that will be addressed within the topic. For example:

 What are the causes of local conflict?

 What are the causes of international conflict?

How are local conflicts resolved?

Students take a double spread and create a page that must include the topic title, key questions and a series of images, cartoons, diagrams and so on that will help them remember the main ideas. As they progress through the topic, they can regularly return to the Big Picture page and add further information and images.

The Connect section can be used at the start of each lesson to connect the learning that is about to happen and could from time to time be used as a review page as students, at the end of a lesson, add new ideas and information dealt with in that lesson.

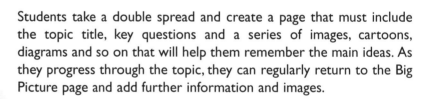 2 Activitate section

This section will be used for the major activity of the lesson. The major activity may be an in-depth study of the Cuban missile crisis and this section of the book could contain appropriate maps, notes, timelines and decisions that students have worked to compile. Reference to the connect page can be made as appropriate.

In the example of the study of local conflict, students may continue, after looking at an introductory video, by considering further case studies of local conflicts and identifying other causes of conflict before discovering the mechanisms available for the resolution of these conflicts. In the activate section of their exercise books, students may record their findings using the method of their choice.

3 Demonstrate section

This section gives students the opportunity to explain their new understanding in relation to a study of the Cuban missile crisis; for example, this might be Beat The Examiner or a simulated press conference resulting in a front page scoop. These are useful techniques if you wish your students to record and retain a body of notes for later revision. (These and other ideas are explored in more depth in the Demonstration phase activities section, pages 36 – 39.)

4 Reviewing our learning section

At the end of a lesson students may be asked, for example, to write down five things they have learned that they did not know at the start of the lesson. Here students can draw and complete their block reviews. They can also review the processes they have been through and reflect on how they have worked. Any review activity you choose can be accommodated here. By collecting the various review methods in this section, students will quickly become familiar with the different ways of reviewing their work.

Smart marking

'Learning is formed more by feedback
than by instruction.'

*In 1998 Professors Black and Wiliam (King's College, London)
published an article detailing their findings from a research
project entitled* Inside the Black Box. *The project focused on
the impact of various assessment strategies on raising
attainment. They found that where assessment was used
formatively, there were significant improvements in attainment.*

The research described in Assessment for Learning: Beyond
the Black Box *completed by the Assessment Reform Group
(1999) concluded that improving learning through assessment
depends on the following five key factors:*

* The provision of effective feedback to students.

* The active involvement of students in their own learning.

* Adjusting teaching to take account of the results of assessment.

* A recognition of the profound influence assessment has on the motivation and self-esteem of students.

* The need for students to be able to assess themselves and understand how to improve.

*Here are some ideas about how Assessment for Learning
principles can underpin, support and enhance each stage of
the Accelerated Learning Cycle.*

Connection phase

'At the heart of Assessment for Learning is the sharing of clear and concise
learning intentions.'
Shirley Clarke (2001)

The starting point for effective lesson planning is the consideration of
learning outcomes. What do I want students to know or be able to
do at the end of 50 minutes with me that they could not do before?

Agree learning outcomes with students, write them on a large piece of flip chart paper and pin them up somewhere prominent in the classroom. Actively involve students in the construction of the learning outcomes. Refer to the outcomes throughout the lesson.

Even better, engage students in extended dialogue about learning outcomes. For example:

Arrange a rope on the floor. At one end it means 'a lot', at the other it means 'nothing'. Ask the question: 'What do you know about Adolf Hitler?' Students stand on the line. Then you ask 'What do you want to know about Adolf Hitler?' Or a variation used by Paul Ginnis is to stick a cross on the floor using masking tape (see Connection phase activities, pages 22–29).

The teacher can then mix groups to include enthusiasts with sceptics, and the ignorant with the well informed. The new groups then generate lots and lots of questions. The questions are then categorized to form broad learning outcomes.

Some schools use **WILF** and **TIBS**.

WILF is symbolized by a goldfish and stands for 'What I'm Looking For' – the teacher makes clear what they are asking for. It could also be **WALT**. **WALT** stands for 'What Are We Learning Today?' This is better because it involves the students more.

TIBS is a large cat and stands for 'This Is Because' – an attempt is made to make the learning relevant to the learner. Students can be greeted by these characters every lesson.

Assessment for Learning is also about 'training' students to be quality assessors and to recognize what constitutes a 'good' piece of work. In this Connection phase the teacher might also engage students in a discussion about 'How will we know we have been successful?' Success criteria should also be agreed and displayed. Look at the following example from a learning to learn lesson.

What I'm Looking For – is for you to practise your concept mapping skills by creating a unique concept map of the information I have given you.

This Is Because – concept mapping is an important technique that will help you to make sense of a large amount of information very quickly.

How will we know we have been successful? This is established with students, that is, a 'quality' concept map would be colourful and contain both keywords and images. Links between topics or ideas would be clearly shown. These would be summarized and posted in the classroom. The teacher might even have had some concept maps that students had completed the year before. Students might have been asked to rank them in order of quality or to select which one they thought best and to explain their choice.

Activation phase

'Most teachers answer their own questions.'

Use open-ended questioning techniques throughout the lesson to get students to think about their work in relation to success criteria. Allow 'think' time. Research has shown that most teachers answer their own questions and the average think time in most classes is between 0.7 and 1.3 seconds. Also teachers rarely plan the questions they will ask during a lesson. Encourage students to ask questions of each other and to pair/share possible answers.

Use grouping effectively and flexibly. Facilitate peer tutoring by placing students who demonstrate a good understanding with those who do not.

Demonstration phase

'Show you know.'

What better way to demonstrate understanding of a topic than by getting students to set tests for each other. Students can work in pairs to identify what they think should be on the test and to generate simple test items and responses. They can then mark tests and feedback to their friends.

Make sure students are only asked to demonstrate understanding in relation to agreed success criteria. For example, if the learning outcome of the lesson was 'By the end of this lesson you will be able to give three examples of a sedimentary rock', it would be unfair to expect students to be able to give a full description of how metamorphic rocks are formed, since you did not tell them.

Consolidation phase

'Allow time for feedback and reflection.'

This is where students can really get involved in feedback. Students could assess each other's presentations and suggest ways in which the presentation could be improved. It is of course important that students are taught how to give feedback sensitively and appropriately. Feedback must relate only to the agreed 'success' criteria. Use a feedback sheet or a scoring template to guide student feedback. Ask them to concentrate on only one aspect of a presentation at first and gradually build up as students get better at assessment and feedback.

This phase also offers an important opportunity for students to reflect on their own work and to make judgements about the quality, perhaps setting themselves targets for future improvement. Self-assessment sheets or learning diaries are useful tools for this. Make sure everyone views self-assessment as a thinking and talking activity and not just as a writing one.

Great ways to make marking smarter

'The single most powerful modification that enhances achievement is feedback. The simplest prescription for improving education must be "dollops of feedback".'

Hattie (1992)

'The research reported here shows conclusively that formative assessment does improve learning. The gains in achievement appear to be quite considerable ... amongst the largest ever noted for educational interventions.'

Black and Wiliam (1998)

The more involved the learner is, the better...

The less work the teacher does, the better...

The nearer the real experience the feedback is, the better...

The more specific the feedback, the better...

The clearer and more readily understood the assessment criteria, the better

SMART MARKING

Our first recommendation is that you remove the word 'marking' from the school vocabulary. Do so immediately! Inform parents that in the past 'marking' was just that: leaving marks to show you had been there. It is the sort of thing mice do when they have been in your kitchen cupboards. Now the school wants to involve learners more and so you will be creating lots of opportunities for improvement through feedback.

In work done by Marzano (2001), teachers who achieved the greatest increase in raising achievement were those who helped students to understand through comparison and classification activities. Try to weave into your feedback strategy lots of opportunities for making comparisons, ordering and providing classification systems.

Criteria first

The criteria for assessment is recorded at the top of a piece of work and before it has been started.

Join the dots

Mistakes are identified by a green dot and no more. The student then makes the correction.

Bullet points for improvement

No more than three very specific bullet points for improvement. The student records them in the back of the book and over time they form the focus for learning review.

Peer marking

Using a 4:1 rubber stamp or paper pro forma – four positive features vs one feature for improvement, a piece of work is given a preliminary evaluation by a peer from within an ability group.

Trial marking

Sample scripts are photocopied and worked on by small groups against criteria described by the teacher. They assign a mark and a rationale for each sample.

Doing it in moderation

As above but this time the scripts are then placed in a rank order.

Critical friends

In pairs and using a set of prompt questions, questions are asked that require the originator of the work to explain what they have done and why. Nothing is written down at this stage and the originator has the opportunity to re-draft.

Hunt for evidence

The teacher provides criteria for success and, in pairs or threes, students search the script for evidence that it is there. In this and in other activities like it, the imperative is to find successes not evidence of failure.

Agree the criteria

Assessment criteria is shared, discussed and then re-written in student-friendly language and presented in a visual reminder.

e-easy way

Groups of students share their draft essays in e-mails. They work in small networked learning communities! Each member of the community has been given a different task so that there is little chance of replication.

Rolling audit

You do not mark every piece of written work but rather audit what is done and every third piece is marked. However, students are on a different marking regime so that you are marking every time you set work but not every student piece that is completed. Those who are on 'hold' work with others in peer-review teams and self-assess by comparing the comments you have made on other scripts. This ensures that there is formative dialogue about work but you are not burning out.

Taxonomy of errors
The teacher provides different categories of errors and these are discussed at length so that marking can be a question of identifying which category. Students can then be tutored in groups against commonly made mistakes.

Tablet PCs
Use tablet PCs with wireless links to record formative assessment of students as you interact with them in lessons. This can then be downloaded and saved for later use – perhaps sent to their e-mail address or made available for individual access with a password on the subject area site.

Pre-drafting
Before written pieces are submitted they are shared in pairs or in supportive small groups and any possible errors corrected there and then.

Give time
In lessons give time for students to respond to written feedback.

Prompts
Help students to improve work with scaffolded prompts, close the gap statements or examples.

Great lesson beginnings

Engage attention in order to direct it.

Adapt these for lessons or for training days. Humour and movement will help capture students' interest.

1 **Question/answer cards.** Students have to find the answer to their question, which is on the reverse of another's question card.

2 **Dense teacher.** Get the class to help you with an obvious problem you 'can't figure out'.

3 **Hunt for autographs.** Pre-prepare a list of attributes/skills for students to match up with classmates and get their autograph.

4 **Time limited brainstorming.** What students know about a new topic against the clock (individual/pair/group).

5 **Three-minute summary.** One student from each group takes exactly three minutes to summarize information for the others.

6 **Press conference.** In groups, students present their information from the sound bite session in summary form. Questions from the floor follow. The event is run along the lines of a press conference.

7 **Post-it parade.** Each pair writes one fact or statement about the topic on a post-it note. Each post-it is placed on the whiteboard. The class then look at each note and classify by re-positioning them on the board.

8 **Milling round.** The class mill around and, on cue, introduce themselves to someone and describe one thing they have learned so far. On cue they swap roles. Each round consists of one minute per pair before a new round begins.

9 **Up in the lift.** Between the first and the tenth floor you have to find out what the other person has been learning that day. It takes 90 seconds for the lift to travel between floors.

10 **Feely bag.** There are five items in the bag that relate to today's lesson. One person puts their hand in the bag and describes what they feel. The others discuss what it might be and how it relates to the topic.

11 **Artefact challenge.** Use to prompt questions and discussions.

LESSON BEGINNINGS

64

section **FOUR**

ACCELERATED LEARNING – A User's Guide

12 Arouse curiosity! At the start of a topic show an object or objects and ask students to guess their use. The same principle can apply to photographs – what do you think is happening? and so on.

13 Intriguing issues! Turn the topic into an intriguing issue. Instead of the 'Today we are going to study the water cycle', which is rather flat and dry, try 'Today we will ask the question – "How can we ensure that everybody on the planet has access to fresh water?"'

14 Give personal meaning. 'Imagine you have woken up today in a world without electricity.' Spend ten minutes writing an account of the next hour of your day.

15 Involve. Show a carefully chosen powerful visual image (slide/photograph), ask students to describe everything they see and then invite some students to 'step into' the slide/photograph and act out what they think is happening. The teacher can pretend to have a microphone and interview the students using well directed questions. The slide(s)/photographs should be clearly tied to your learning objectives, illustrate key events/issues/concepts, have the potential for students to step into and act out, and be fun or unusual.

16 The ambassador's reception. The scene is a sophisticated ambassador's reception, classical music plays. Students circulate chatting to each other about the highlights from the previous lesson. They carry an appointments card on which is written four deliberately provocative statements related to the topic about to be studied. On one side of the card is a picture of a clock with spaces to write in appointments at 3 o'clock, 6 o'clock, 9 o'clock and 12 o'clock. When the music stops, students turn to the person nearest to them and discuss the first statement. The teacher allows a few minutes for them to do this and then warns that the music is about to start again. At this point, students write each other's names in the 3 o'clock appointment slot and agree to see each other later. The music starts and students once again move off into the social swirl. The teacher stops the music again a little while later and students repeat the exercise – this time discussing the second statement before finally making a 6 o'clock appointment. This continues until each student has discussed four statements and made four appointments that they will later keep throughout the lesson or at some future time. Each of the statements they have been discussing have stimulated thought about the learning to come and you have cleverly set up four different pairings for pair/share work later in the lesson.

17 Humour. Stick an OHP of a humorous cartoon connected to the topic in some way on the board. The internet is a great source for these.

18 Let there be music. Choose a suitable and contextualizing piece of music or song either to create the mood or to provide a context for the learning to come. Use irony; for example, 'Another Day in Paradise' by Phil Collins at the beginning of a module on homelessness, or Blondie's 'Atomic' at the beginning of a lesson on the structure of the atom.

19 Overhead projector silhouette. Place an object to do with the lesson on an OHP so students can see only the silhouette. Ask students in pairs to guess what the object is and what it may have to do with today's lesson.

20 Turn up on, or ahead of, time!

Great classroom motivators

'Motivation is emotion in motion.'

1 Sell the benefits. Explain what we all gain from the outcomes of the learning. What makes us better off by doing this?

2 Share the process. Explain the methodology for learning.

3 Being esteemed by an influencer. The basic unit of motivational currency is the interest of another human. Show your interest.

4 Educative feedback. Give specific bullet points for improvement that can be acted on there and then.

5 Praise that is private and personal not public and paraded is the best for many – especially truculent boys.

6 Proximity modelling. Role-model close at hand. Do not pretend we can all bend it like Beckham if we try hard enough. We might be able to bash it like Bloggs and take it from there.

7 Chunked challenges. A little and often is the best way to improve. What one per cent improvement steps are available for our GCSE coursework? Identify the one per cent steps.

8 Little acts of kindness. Give something of value away to the most difficult student and expect nothing in return. A copy of the *Angler's Mail* may be enough to change the relationship with the hostile boy who loves fishing.

9 Security of a ritual. In threat, a ritual makes us feel safe. In high challenge, ritualized, shared moments help you cope.

10 Two-dimensional debriefing. Debrief tests and mock exams for knowledge and feelings. This lets students know that everyone gets stressed in an exam. And besides, they are more interested in the feelings dimension.

11 Provide meaningful choice in lessons.

At the end of the day students will engage in a lesson if:

 the topic is intrinsically interesting.
 the topic is relevant – students can see some purpose.
a connection (or connections) can be made.
the students like you – relationships are important and take time to build.

66

Great ways to get into groups

'Learning is a social activity enhanced by shared enquiry.'

1 Group-work protocols throughout the school.
Agree and put into your staff handbook protocols for group
working that every teacher can readily use. By doing so it is made
easier for students and staff alike.

2 Group-work protocol for your classroom. Agree
simple protocols for moving into and between groups and display
these prominently.

3 Home and away groups. Home groups are friendship
groups with high levels of familiarity. Away groups are non-
friendship groups with lower levels of familiarity.

4 Group roles. Assign groups roles and have laminated
cards that outline what students do in each nominated role.

5 Groupings by purpose.

6 Random selection.

7 Mixed ability grouping.

8 Press corps. A group whose job it is to report on the
activities and progress of other groups. A press conference
of findings can then follow.

9 Envoys. Each group sends an envoy to each of the
other groups to share findings, information or to gather it.

10 Building up and scaling down. Pairs go into
fours, then eights.

Suggested group roles

The Co-ordinator
With responsibility for making sure everyone in the group
understands the task in hand, becomes involved in decision making
and takes on a role in the generation of solutions or outcomes.

The Cartographer
With responsibility for recording decisions which have been agreed.

The Clockwatcher
With responsibility for ensuring the activity and its component
stages are completed within time.

The Collector
With responsibility for obtaining any resources that will be needed.

The Checker
With responsibility for ensuring that what is planned actually occurs.

The Communicator
With responsibility for talking to other groups and for summarizing findings.

Good questions for group members to ask

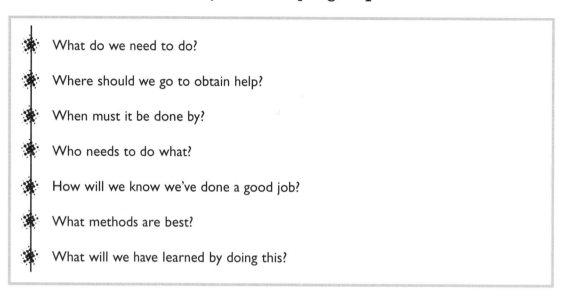

* What do we need to do?

* Where should we go to obtain help?

* When must it be done by?

* Who needs to do what?

* How will we know we've done a good job?

* What methods are best?

* What will we have learned by doing this?

How to get quiet

'I will not yell she's dead during roll call.
I will not sleep through my education.
I will not grease the wall bars.
I will not dissect things without instructions.'
Matt Groenig, Bart's blackboard lines, The Simpsons

1 Carpet the classroom.

2 Teach appropriate 'sound levels for learning' as a whole-class activity and practise them.

3 Teach 'good listening' skills.

4 Avoid seeing silence as necessarily purposeful and always conducive to learning.

5 Provide lots of opportunity for structured paired and small group discussion.

6 Lower your voice.

7 Ensure all new furniture has rubber tips on the bottom! Buy blinds that roll rather than pull vertically.

8 Replace chalkboards with whiteboards.

shhhhhh...

9 Use a noise meter visual to show what sort of volume level is appropriate for any given activity.

10 Play quiet, restful background music and gradually lower the volume.

11 Play 'natural sounds', such as birdsong, quietly as background!

12 Practise extended visualization as part of classroom learning.

13 Review lesson content using a passive concert: students close their eyes, rest their heads and listen as you review the key material with quiet background music.

14 Give the very young fidgeters noiseless 'toys' to fidget with, so they do not distract everyone else.

15 Use quality audience – agree with the class the criteria for a top quality audience. Put these up on the classroom wall and thereafter pre-signal your request for a quality audience by saying 'Can I have a quality audience in five seconds please – 5-4-3-2-1. Quality audience now please.' Hold hand in air to back this up with a physical signal. Be persistent; this is important.

16 Use your position in class. For example, always stand in the same place in the classroom when asking for quiet. Pretty soon your class will start to associate your moving to this particular spot with a signal for quiet.

17 Establish important classroom rituals. For example, we always start lessons by reviewing what we learned from last time. When someone else is talking, everyone puts down their pens and listens.

How to use physical reprieve

'Stasis fatigue: immobilized for too long.'

1 Recognize that no one is good at sitting still for extended periods of time. Do not expect the class to be able to sit with focused attention for long periods of time.

2 Try to make diffusion part of the lesson. For example, a short, timed review where students cross the room and describe to someone else three things they have already learned.

3 Adopt a focus–diffuse–focus–diffuse model for engaging and diffusing attention and for building in short structured breaks.

4 As a crude rule of thumb (with no basis in science!), use the chronological age plus one maxim: for focused attention for 10 year olds work to 11 or 12 minutes before a diffusion.

5 Practise stretching exercises regularly.

6 Use modelling and physical learning – number lines, continuity lines, body sculptures, living graphs – as an integral part of your lesson.

7 Familiarize yourself with brain-break activities and their different applications.

8 Practise classroom yoga, deep breathing and relaxation techniques with your class; incorporate this into mental rehearsals of learning.

9 Plan in at least two short breaks for every hour of classroom teaching.

10 Keep fit yourself.

focus

diffuse

diffuse

focus

Great ways to use music

'Music will energize or relax, aid long-term memory and recall, influence behaviour and manage mood.'

1 Only use music to aid learning and be clear in your own mind how using music in your classroom aids learning.

2 Choose the music yourself and have only one source of music, that is, no personal stereos.

3 Categorize the music by learning purpose: energizing, relaxing, focusing, themed, timed task and visualization.

4 Discuss how and why music is used to aid learning; find out who enjoys learning to music and who finds it distracting.

5 Use calming music for starting lessons.

6 Learn key concepts through learning songs; use familiar tunes to help.

7 Devise learning songs as a whole-class activity starting with keywords.

8 Take familiar songs and replace some of the words with your own keywords.

9 Use music to signify celebratory and/or ritual events such as an end of unit quiz.

10 Use music on entry to tests and exams to provide a sense of familiarity and to relax.

11 Use music to create a mood; for example, 'Eye of the Tiger' from the film *Rocky* for challenge.

12 Use music as a timing device; for example, the theme from *Mission Impossible* for clearing up.

Watch your language

> 'If there's one word that sums up everything that's
> gone wrong since the war, it's "workshop".'
> Kingsley Amis (1980)

The language that is used in classrooms plays a part in shaping the experience of user and receiver. Here are a few suggestions for monitoring your classroom talk.

1 Teacherese! Words such as 'woe betide' are never heard except in a classroom! There is a vocabulary that should be redundant but continues to be used in classrooms. Adding to the confusion is the occasional tendency to indulge in ambiguities: 'What do we not do when we go to assembly?' 'Can we take our coats off now please?' Evidence shows that the subsequent confusion can contribute to misbehaviour.

2 Avoid too much 'Yes but' thinking. If you are predisposed to find fault, it will be reflected in your choice of words. 'I agree with you, however' has a very different impact to 'I agree with you and.'

3 Use choice drivers. Choose to say, 'Alistair what will you do with your mobile? Switch it off and put it away or give it to me to look after for you?' rather than 'Put it away or else!'

4 Superfluous questions! 'Now do you all understand?' 'Have we all finished yet?' 'How are we all getting on?' These are not very useful and amount to mere noise.

5 Try language sandwiches! Sandwich positive and negative statements in different combinations to see which work best for you: 'We are making good progress. I notice that you have not yet completed the exercise. I'm confident you'll succeed before the end of the lesson.' This is a positive–negative–positive sandwich.

6 Use more of the word 'learning'. 'Let's get on with our learning.' Is more attractive and more useful than 'Let's get on with our work.'

7 Avoid overusing the word 'marking'. Replace it with the word 'feedback'.

8 Avoid overusing the word 'ability'. Replace it with the word 'abilities'.

9 Use 'noticing' language. You describe in objective terms a student's learning behaviour. 'I noticed that when I introduced this topic there were lots of good questions which

LANGUAGE

included ...' You can then invite thoughts as to why this was noteworthy.

10 Use 'earshotting'. This simple technique involves deliberately letting someone hear you make positive comments about them within earshot. You are speaking to someone else but know that even if what you said is not heard, it will be passed on.

11 Use future focus and not past prejudice. Because someone behaved in a given way yesterday, it should not hold their behaviour to ransom today. By choosing to use a language of possibility – 'What would it be like if?' 'How might you do this differently?' 'When you've perfected it, what will it be like?' – you can effect positive changes in behaviour.

12 Match predicates. This is a NLP technique involving matching of language preference to improve rapport between two parties. Visual processing is often reflected in the use of visual predicates – 'I see what you mean', 'It looks good to me' and others. Auditory processing is sounded out in the use of auditory predicates – 'I hear what you are saying', 'It started alarm bells ringing for me' and others. Kinesthetic processing is often reflected in the use of kinesthetic predicates – 'It feels fine', 'It moved me' and others. When talking to students listen carefully to the words they use and match with those that are similar.

13 Say what you want, rather than say what you don't want. This makes everyday dialogue easier. For example, if you have specified what good listening behaviour is like, you can catch it more easily when you get it.

LANGUAGE

Visual display

> 'The brain is firstly an image processor before it is a word processor.'

1 Learning posters

Create very large, easy-to-read posters that summarize the essential learning points and place them in a space on your classroom wall. Laminate the posters in matt so they can be used again and again. Test students' recall of the posters. Have them record the poster in a revision book and practise mentally rehearsing the look of the poster. Move the laminated learning posters and the vocabulary of related words into the corridor space.

2 Related vocabulary in families

Surround the learning poster with related vocabulary. Never place key vocabulary in rows. Try to link it to the content of the learning poster through its physical spacing. Use the connecting words to develop understanding of key concepts.

3 Learning behaviours

Use cryptic descriptors of useful learning behaviours. For example, 'Getting stuck is not a problem, staying stuck is. Good learners practise getting unstuck.' These can be themed, form the topic for class lessons and appear on websites, screen savers and in the parents' newsletter.

4 Poster rehearsals

Learning posters and their families of related keywords are used as core revision material in advance of public tests and exams.

5 Interactive displays

If students' work is to be displayed, make its display significant by drawing attention to it. Position it in public places. Make it interactive so that close scrutiny is required and rewarded. Do not stick it up through force of habit, or for wallpaper, or for any purpose other than one that supports learning.

6 Passports to success

Success criteria should be displayed prominently. Smaller, laminated, playing card versions of the summary criteria posters should be made available and used as classroom prompt cards. Because they are small, students can keep their own. They can be used as the basis of classroom activities.

7 Electronic whiteboards

An electronic whiteboard should be more than a large visual aid. Use it as you would any other significant learning resource. Optimize student access and use.

8 Steps to success

Use prominent visual displays of steps necessary to improve performance in, say, creative writing. Reinforce by students having their own versions recorded in a workbook.

9 Using an OHP

Use colour on your transparencies. Prepare them beforehand so that you can incorporate images. Encourage students to get used to using it for simple and effective summaries of group findings, topics that have been learned and points of view. With a visual prompt it is easier for any student to talk through their findings in a coherent way. Be creative!

An English teacher made a silhouette for a session on Shakespearean sonnets by placing a single rose on an OHP – she then introduced the topic against a backdrop of a single rose, the effect was quite mesmerizing. (You could do a 'guess what the objects are' as a way of 'hooking' your audience into a topic.)

10 Thinking wall

Build up 'thinking' culture in your classroom by having a large Bloom's taxonomy display on one wall with associated thinking vocabulary for each level of thinking (page 23). For example, for knowledge, the lowest level on the thinking ladder, you could have the words 'repeat', 'recall' and so on written on pieces of card stuck to the wall. Throughout the lesson students could be asked to indicate what level of 'thinking' is taking place.

VISUAL
DISPLAY

Using technology

'The technology tail should not wag the learning dog.'

A structured model for engaging learning becomes even more important when there is a proliferation of information technologies in and around classrooms. Here are some considerations:

1 Is it safe! There is no 'right' technology. It is simply right for the purpose at this moment in time. At one stage, the two-colour banda (spirit-based duplication machine) was the height of resource sophistication.

2 Impress me! Expensive technology brings pressure on staff to quickly show expertise in its use. Prepare for this by planning the training before installation. Do not delegate the training to the suppliers!

3 Nerd creep. Love of the technology for its own sake exerts a negative pressure on good teaching and squeezes it out.

4 Ability divides. Disparities in staff use and understanding of the classroom applications of the technology will quickly widen.

5 Changing looms! Hover technology was going to change the world in the late 1960s. Apart from the Flymo, it never did. Do not put all your investment into one type of technology.

6 Curriculum lag. The curriculum is not re-thought as quickly as the technology is.

7 Fit for purpose. Use a balance of technology that is fit for purpose – rather than put all your eggs in one expensive basket.

8 FiFi. Fit it, Forget it! Avoid installing expensive technology and then forgetting it. Review its use and influence regularly.

9 Piles. Avoid piling new learning and teaching demands on top of an old model of what is needed.

10 Total cost of ownership. Factor in training costs – time and personnel – when devising your technology strategy.

11 Think loopy. Think of classwork, private study and homework as a loop system.

TECHNOLOGY

12 Mind the gap. Use technology to decrease the gaps between home and school, community and school, the world and school.

13 Whose technology? Consider how the technology actively and meaningfully engages the learner; investigate its use by structured classroom observation. Ask who uses it and when? How does it influence classroom interactions? What happens to problem solving? Discussion? How does differentiation exhibit itself?

14 Plan for the novelty wearing off ...

Using ICT to support Accelerated Learning

'It is not the size of your RAM that is important but how you use your equipment.'

What is ICT?

ICT stands for Information and Communication Technology. It is not just about computers but any piece of technology that supports or enables communication: from mobile phones to DVD players, from OHPs to tape recorders. You do not have to have the latest and most expensive equipment or the greatest number of 'megapixels' to use ICT effectively in the classroom.

Getting started – the basic equipment for the twenty-first-century classroom

Ideally every learning space will have the following:

At least one computer (PC) with a link to the internet (world wide web) or to school intranet (internal network).

A pair of speakers so you have access to sound – we are always amazed at how many people forget about sound. Speakers are fairly cheap – about £10.

A microphone that fits into the PC – this allows you or your students to create sound files and to use brilliant pieces of software like Camtasia (see opposite).

A cheap digital camera – the ones that are most useful in the classroom are the most basic ones with a floppy disk that clicks into the back. Do not play the 'megapixels' game and buy a fancy camera that comes with its own software.

Access to a printer – this does not mean every room has to have a printer, but reasonable access is important. Get a robust black and white printer for regular use. Colour does make a huge difference and the printers themselves are not expensive but the replacement colour cartridges when you run out of ink are.

If your budget runs to it, then an interactive whiteboard or a portable data projector makes a big difference in the classroom and opens up a whole range of possibilities. If your budget does not, then buy a lead that connects your computer to a television screen. This is a much cheaper alternative and, importantly, allows you to display what is on the computer screen to the whole class.

Six must-have pieces of software

Inspiration (or for younger students Kidspiration) – this piece of software allows the user to combine keywords and images to create 'concept' or thinking maps.

Camtasia – this piece of software 'videos' the computer screen as you work on it and records your voice as you explain what you are doing.

PowerPoint – an excellent presentational software. If used effectively, it can be highly visual and engaging. It is a good tool for supporting student presentations, allowing them to talk through and explain their work and ideas.

Hot Potatoes – free software (download from internet) that allows the user to create a range of drag and drop or multiple response tests.

Sound forge – this piece of software allows you to record and edit sound files with ease.

And don't forget Word for Windows – few people make full use of this piece of software. For example, you can attach sound files to bring the text to life or use the 'Insert' function to add comment boxes that appear automatically when the cursor moves over a particular word. You can also add hypertext links that automatically take the user to relevant websites at the click of a button or simply use the highlight function to select keywords in different colours.

How can ICT support the Accelerated Learning Cycle?

Outlined below are a few examples of how ICT can support each part of the four-stage Accelerated Learning Cycle – it is by no means exhaustive but should provide a useful starting point.

Connection Phase

Set up a PowerPoint presentation containing keywords and images from the previous lesson or series of lessons. Set the slides to 'scroll' – that is, to automatically fade through black and move onto the next slide every five seconds. Add a contextualizing piece of music or just an upbeat piece of music. You now have a highly engaging start to the lesson that reminds students about the work they have been doing as they come through the classroom door.

Drag and drop 'bellwork' – students use an interactive whiteboard pen to drag and drop labels onto a diagram or to match keywords with definitions. The first student through the door gets the whiteboard pen and after they have dragged and dropped the first label they get to choose who goes next. This ensures that every one is on their toes.

Use Google search 'image' to access pictures connected to any topic almost instantaneously. If the connection is tenuous, even better; get students to suggest the possible link to what they have been studying.

Spice up a presentation of new information with an online video; for example, a two-minute clip showing black and white footage of Buzz Aldrin on the Moon or a live recording of Martin Luther King in action.

Activation Phase

This is where the student can be making good use of ICT. If you only have one PC in the classroom, then arrange a carousel of activities around the room and make ICT one of them. Students could work in groups of four and spend ten minutes at each 'learning' zone before moving on.

ICT activities could range from:

students creating their own PowerPoint that they will use later to present their ideas to other students. Or they might create a set of annotated PowerPoint slides that other students can use as a learning resource. They could use 'sound forge' software and a microphone to add audio buttons to record their thoughts out loud.

students visiting a number of websites set up by the teacher. They use an online graphic organizer to compare and contrast the information they find on each website.

students using an online writing template to help organize their thoughts. For example, a 'newspaper' front page is already set up with keyword prompts to help students get started.

students watching a Camtasia tutorial set up by the teacher that takes them through a problem-solving exercise; for example, in maths before they try to solve some similar questions.

students using a digital camera to provide a visual document of their work in progress – they can use it later to explain their thinking at each stage of their design process.

students using plasticine to make simple models of the stages of a physical process; for example, tectonic plates colliding – they label and photograph each stage with a digital camera, then use Paintshop Pro to edit a short animated sequence to explain what is happening.

Demonstration Phase

Many of the activities described above can also be used to give students the opportunity to demonstrate their new understanding. Here are a few more.

Students answer an online test or quiz that the teacher has prepared (using Hot Potatoes) earlier. Tests can be set up to be self-marking and to give students immediate feedback.

Students prepare an online test for their classmates (using Hot Potatoes) to complete – they have to know the answers to be able to do this.

Students use Inspiration to create a concept map that summarizes their understanding of a topic or module. The concept map mixes images and key ideas and clearly shows the connections between various parts of the topic.

Students use Camtasia to produce an online tutorial for fellow classmates; for example, talking their way through a problem they have solved or interpreting a piece of text from a play.

Consolidation Phase

The teacher has **a skeletal concept map** on an interactive whiteboard. The teacher talks through and adds connections to the map in discussion with students.

The teacher has produced **a concept map** giving an overview of the whole topic. This is printed out and students work in pairs to highlight the areas they still need to ask about or to add information they feel has been missed out.

The teacher takes **digital photographs** of students during group-work – these are now on screen and the teacher uses them to discuss process with the students; for example, 'How do we know this group is working really well together?' 'Can you explain what you were thinking at this point?'

Scroll PowerPoint with keywords, images and pictures of students working to summarize and reinforce key learning points from the lesson.

Using ICT as a planning tool for staff

By creating an online lesson planning tool for staff, all lessons can be planned online and easily updated. They are also available for anyone to use, including supply staff, and resources for the lesson can be linked to the lesson plan so that they are a mere click of a mouse button away. Overleaf is an example that shows how one school has interpreted the four-stage Accelerated Learning Cycle to create an online lesson planning template that puts good practice in the right order and makes it explicit.

Blank lesson planning pro forma

Timing		
Connect the Learning		
The Big Picture		
Share the Learning *Outcomes* *Content* *Skills Thinking*	**By the end of this lesson you will be able to**	**Bloom's Taxonomy Flip Chart** *6 Evaluation* *5 Synthesis* *4 Analysis* *3 Application* *2 Comprehension* *1 Knowledge*
Introduce New Information *VAK (OG)*		
Activity *Multiple Intelligences* *Higher Order Thinking Skills (HOTS)* *Closed/Open* ––––––––––––– *teacher student* *directed constructed* *Opportunities for ICT?*		
Demonstrate Your New Understanding *Opportunities for ICT?*		
Review/Debrief/Preview *Opportunities for ICT?*		
Assessment for Learning		
Home Learning *Opportunities for ICT?*		
Resources		

Lessons are either 55 minutes or 110 minutes

Relevant music or video clip or key questions or task 'loaded' in advance for instant access

These can be negotiated with the class if desired. Learning outcomes are cross references against the appropriate level of Bloom's taxonomy

The interactive whiteboard is ideal for this section

Constant reminders to integrate ICT in the lesson!

'Homework' is integrated into the planning process

The completed pro forma would appear to the whole class via the interactive whiteboard. Links to internet and intranet are 'built in' and accessible at the touch of the whiteboard pen. Each stage of the cycle can be 'blanked off' if it is felt undesirable to show it to the class in advance.

Designing Accelerated Learning web pages

'There are now more pages of information on the world wide web than there are people on the planet.'

1 First ask the question 'Is my content suited to an interactive medium?' Most 'so called' learning websites consist of worksheets, scanned text and out-of-date links. Is this really what you want?

2 Next, ask the question 'If I took the content of my website and taught it as a live lesson, would I leave the room proud of what I had achieved?'

3 Do not delude yourself that because it is on a screen it is somehow better!

4 Always apply the KISS of (learning) life to any online content: keep it simple stupid!

5 Use the Accelerated Learning Cycle to help structure your design. This ensures you build in connecting activities, each input comprises different visual, auditory and tactile stimulus, there are opportunities to demonstrate understanding and a consolidation review.

6 Never paste in whole pages of text and leave it. Learning online requires more summaries, more visuals, more reflective questions and more navigation cues.

7 Site your pages within navigation windows so that the learner can immediately see where they are and how it links to the Bigger Picture.

8 Research suggests that a learner can easily manage three windows open at any one time. You can have a main window with your body text, a vertical right-hand side window that carries short summaries, visuals and links, and a top horizontal window that shows where the learner is on the site.

9 Use an open, easily readable and modern-looking font that is consistent throughout your website. Avoid changing fonts unnecessarily.

10 Avoid words like work, test, study, concentration and effort in your guidance and replace with a vocabulary that is more appropriate to an online experience: learning, review, access, share, celebrate, scorecard, browse, broker, chat, search, spam, download, upgrade, portal and conference.

11 Use recurring and recognizable icons for: summary, must know, keywords, self-test questions, picture gallery and sample answers.

12 Do not use more than three basic colours on any one page.

13 Work on a ratio of one visual to every 250 words. At the very least break the text every 250 words.

14 Place visuals and highlighted quotes on the right-hand side of the page.

15 Offer a one-paragraph summary at the beginning of a body of text and place it on the upper right-hand side.

16 Preview the key learning and key vocabulary at the beginning of the text.

17 Within the text, link key vocabulary to definitions so that one click will bring up the meaning of the word.

18 Alongside each visual have a question. By clicking on the visual or the question the learner obtains a linked answer.

19 Have separate picture gallery pages so that visual learners can go through a picture trail and experience the information in a picture sequence.

20 Avoid meaningless activities that do not need a computer – wordsearches, crosswords or cloze – unless they are interactive and integral to your learning outcomes.

21 Time how long it takes you to read through the text and do the activities yourself. For every eight minutes you take, build in a recommended break for your online learner, who by then will have spent at least 20 minutes staring, headlocked at a screen.

22 Make each of these learning breaks part of the learning or a rewarding and fun, physical activity.

Examples of Accelerated Learning lesson plans

'No one is stopped in the street by a grateful ex-student keen to thank you for a memorable worksheet.'

The following lessons have been planned using a planning template based on the four-stage learning cycle.

L2L   Lesson: 25/26
Topic: Concept maps
Timing: x 2 lessons

Resources

- Coloured pens
- A3 paper
- Revision books

CONNECT	
Create the learning environment *That is, display, language, groups, mood, furniture.*	*Display an A3 concept map you have produced or examples from our intranet.*
Connect *To connect learning to previous lesson, or to individual's prior experience, or to stimulate thinking about learning to come (2/3 min activity at beginning of lesson).*	*Get students to compare concept maps they have already done or ask them to write down what they think are the most important points to remember when designing a concept map.*
Agree the learning outcomes/Big Picture first *What will students be able to do at the end of the lesson that they could not do at the beginning?* *How does this 'chunk' of learning fit into whole topic/context?* *(within 5 mins of start of lesson)*	**What I'm Looking For** *is for you to practise your concept mapping skills by creating a unique concept map of the information your teacher will give you.* **This Is Because** *concept mapping is an important revision technique that will help you to make sense of a great deal of information as you prepare for your SATs exams.*

ACTIVATE

Introduction (VAK) ❋ *New information/scene setting/stimulus/hook* ❋ *Through as many of the senses as possible* *(max 10 mins)*	*Go through with the class what a successful concept map looks like and reinforce some of the important points from the teacher's notes. If you are able to, come up with your own concept map for a topic in your own subject area and show students one you 'made earlier'.*
	If you are in a room with an interactive whiteboard and you are familiar with Inspiration, then show students an Inspiration concept map you made earlier and use it to emphasize what makes a good concept map and how it can be useful.
Activities *The search for meaning* ❋ *Use multiple intelligences* ❋ *Are chunked* ❋ *Review learning between each activity* *(Main part of lesson)*	*Students use science revision books to choose a topic and to construct a concept map from the information.* *Produce a draft map first, then whole-class review. Next produce final best effort.*

DEMONSTRATE

Show you know *An opportunity for students to demonstrate their new understanding* *(Main part of lesson)*	*Produce your 'best' concept map and use 'washing line' for display. Students select the best concept map from their table and peg it to a clothes line that is stretched across classroom at front. They must be able to justify their group choice.*

CONSOLIDATE

Review *Reflect* *Recall* *– not just what you learned but how you learned it.*	*Pair/share your concept map with a partner explaining the connections between items as you trace your finger across your concept map (pole-bridging).*

L2L Lesson: _____

Topic: Salt

Timing: Double lesson

example

Resources

- Box of sea salt – any other props; for example, packet of salted crisps, can of Heinz baked beans and so on
- Hand lenses to look at salt
- Bag of sugar for comparison and melt test (looks the same but behaves differently)
- Mini whiteboards for immediate (individual) feedback
- Crucibles, heatproof mats, goggles, Bunsen burners for melt test
- Straw, Sellotape, card and marker pens for puppet show
- Software used – PowerPoint, 'new media' science software

CONNECT

Create the learning environment *That is, display, language, groups, mood, furniture.*	*Tables arranged for groups of 4/5. Students given name badges on entry to classroom.*
Connect *To connect learning to previous lesson, or to individual's prior experience, or to stimulate thinking about learning to come (2/3 min activity at beginning of lesson).*	*On the electronic whiteboard there is a scrolling PowerPoint of pictures that are obscurely to do with salt; for example, picture of a salt mine fades into picture of salted bag of crisps. Students are asked to guess what the topic for the lesson might be from the picture 'clues'.*
Agree the learning outcomes/Big Picture first * What will students be able to do at the end of the lesson that they could not do at the beginning? * How does this 'chunk' of learning fit into whole topic/context? *(within 5 mins of start of lesson)*	**What I'm Looking For** *is students to begin to understand the chemistry of salt and the nature of an ionic bond. Also to see that chemistry can be an interesting and relevant subject and to leave them hungry for more.* **This Is Because** *salt forms a large part of our diet, it is in nearly everything we eat – crisps, baked beans and so on. Salt is all around us – look at the world's oceans, full of salt!* *Take feedback from pair/share discussions – what do students think lesson is about and why. Help them towards the correct answer (if necessary) and produce a bag of sea salt. Give each student a little to look at (can use hand-held lenses), feel, taste. Ask them to draw it on mini whiteboards.* *Ask students what they might like to find out about salt?* *Ask students why it might be interesting or important to find out something about salt?* *Specfic learning outcomes (and success criteria – how will we know we can do this?) are built up with the class and written on a large sheet of flip chart paper that is then displayed in a prominent area in the classroom.*

ACTIVATE

Introduction (VAK)

New information/scene setting/stimulus/hook
Through as many of the senses as possible

(max 10 mins)

Activities

The search for meaning
Use multiple intelligences
Are chunked
Review learning between each activity

(Main part of lesson)

Experiment – melt test

Students compare physical properties of salt with something quite similar; for example, sugar. They discover that although they look the same (both white/crystalline solids) there are differences – taste for one, but more importantly I want them to carry out a melt test to establish that salt does not melt (high melting point) while sugar melts easily. Why? (10 mins)
To understand this we have to look a little closer – at an atomic level and find out what salt is made of and how it is held together. Introduce sodium and chlorine. Be dramatic: sodium soft grey metal I can cut with a knife that 'explodes' on contact with water; chlorine pale yellow, green and poisonous gas. Follow this with a whole-class presentation using new media software to explore salt at atomic level and to explain ionic bond.
(10 mins)

DEMONSTRATE

Show you know

An opportunity for students to demonstrate their new understanding
(Main part of lesson)

Puppet show challenge

You have been asked to create a puppet show to explain the chemistry of salt to young children (8 year olds). You will need to make your puppet show engaging and interesting to hold their attention. The children do, however, also need to learn some important information about the chemistry of salt – you will have to use your puppet show to explain some quite difficult ideas in a way which they can understand. The above challenge is written on a large sheet of flip chart paper and displayed to the class. There is a discussion to make sure students understand exactly what they need to do, what materials are available and when they need to to be ready for presentation.
(15 mins)

CONSOLIDATE

Review
Reflect
Recall

– not just what you learned but how you learned it.

Take pictures of puppet shows taking shape – use these pictures (post them on electronic whiteboard) to lead whole-class discussion returning to some of the fundamental learning points from lesson. Ask students to explain their thinking. (10 mins) Finally get students to complete two sticky notes (different colours) – on one write 'something I found interesting and did not know' and on the other 'one question I still have'.

L2L Lesson: _____
Topic: Skim 'n Scan
Timing: 2 lessons

example

Resources

* Sun information sheet for information retrieval exercise
* Reactivity series for second go at information retrieval
* Envelopes containing articles on Minamata disaster for skim reading exercise
* A3 information organizer sheets for scanning exercise x 8

CONNECT

Create the learning environment *That is, display, language, groups, mood, furniture.*	*The two main activities in these lessons are 'group-work' and 'debrief' - changing the furniture to facilitate these different activities will be useful if this is possible.*
Connect *To connect learning to previous lesson, or to individual's prior experience, or to stimulate thinking about learning to come. (2/3 min activity at beginning of lesson)*	*Rearrange the following two sentences so they make sense:* **Skim** *rapidly general for impression a main the ideas of look through text* **Scan** *rapidly text from by locating out pick words information specific key*
Agree the learning outcomes/Big Picture first ❋ *What will students be able to do at the end of the lesson which they could not do at the beginning?* ❋ *How does this 'chunk' of learning fit into whole topic/context?* *(within 5 mins of start of lesson)*	*The object of the next two lessons is to introduce the students to SKIM and SCAN reading techniques, which will be useful throughout their school life and when reading exam questions. By the end of the next two lessons you will be able to confidently use SCAN and SKIM reading techniques on a variety of texts to find out useful information quickly.* *NB:* *we have tried to choose information that will also help you to prepare for your SATs exam.*

ACTIVATE

Introduction (VAK) ❋ *New information/scene setting/stimulus/hook* ❋ *Through as many of the senses as possible* *(max 10 mins)*	*Information retrieval – this exercise is a thinking skills activity. Students are in teams of four and are numbered 1 to 4. Each group has a blank sheet of A3 paper in front of them and the challenge will be to replicate the information the teacher has on a covered piece of paper at the front of the classroom. Number '1s' are called to the front and allowed to 'view' information for 30 seconds before it is covered up – they return to seat and share info with group for 2 mins before number '2s' are called up and so on.*

Activities	Debrief the process – what strategies did the group employ to access all the information in the given time? What helped them to do this in the way the information was laid out? That is, keywords underlined or in bold, colour, pictures, layout, headings, sub headings, and so on. Does this have any implications for the way they prepare or lay out notes as they get ready for exams for example? Using what they have learned from this debrief, students are now going to have another go but this time will be trying to replicate slightly more complicated information – preview this activity by suggesting they first discuss strategy in their groups.
The search for meaning *Use multiple intelligences* *Are chunked* *Review learning between each activity* (Main part of lesson)	
	Repeat the exercise using the 'reactivity' series page (science revision books).
	Quickly review the exercise – was this more difficult? If so, why? What key information were they looking for (scanning)? Or did they just try to get a general overview very quickly (skimming)? Or did they do a combination of both?

DEMONSTRATE

Show you know *An opportunity for students to demonstrate their new understanding* (Main part of lesson)	In this next exercise students will try to demonstrate use of both techniques. Give each group of four an envelope containing articles on Minamata disaster. 1 Skim info to get general overview. 2 Answer as many questions as possible on A3 information sheet. 3 List/identify what you still need to know. 4 Scan articles for specific information. 5 Add this information to sheet. 6 Write short newspaper article (after agreeing what it might include).
Review *Reflect* *Recall* *– not just what you learned but how you learned.*	Debrief the lesson – 'circle time' Where might students use the skills they have learned? Can they give specific examples of where these skills have or would have been useful in other curriculum areas? How might they change exam preparation techniques in light of this experience and so on? Over the next two weeks ask students to practise the skills of scanning and skimming as many times as possible in other subject areas.

Your questions answered

'Be expedient in strategy and consistent in principles.'

Q

Wasn't all this around in the 1960s and 1970s?

A

Certainly we have been talking about different labels such as 'active learning', 'flexible learning environments', 'taking into account individual needs' for many years now but the Accelerated Learning framework has taken things much further. First, it is based on scientific theories about why things work, including understanding of how the brain functions (for example, high challenge but low threat) as well as what motivates learners. Second, it puts disparate ideas into a very effective sequence of activities (the stages in the cycle) that bring a coherence, pace and rigour to our preparation. With the cycle as a framework or planning vehicle, we get good practice put into the right order.

Q

Isn't this all a restriction on the way teachers teach?

A

Well one would hope that all teachers plan and structure their lessons. You would also hope that this planning and structure would be based on something tangible, like how effective learning happens! If so, the framework will provide a particularly useful support structure. But of course that is only the start. The teacher has absolute freedom to draw on their full repertoire of teaching strategies in order to make effective learning happen. Nobody is telling teachers that they must use techniques such as mind mapping, role play, collaborative learning, and so on. That is left to their professional judgement. Asking which teaching technique is best is analogous to asking which tool is best – a hammer, a screwdriver, a knife or pliers. In teaching, as in carpentry, the selection of tools depends on the task at hand and the materials one is working with. It follows that the more tools you have in your toolbox and the more you understand and appreciate their use, the more likely you are to get the job done. And some classes on some days, as well as some individuals, require a very specialized spanner!

Q

Does this mean that whole-class 'traditional' teaching is wrong?

A

Of course not. Book work and lectures CAN be wonderfully efficient modes of transmitting new information for learning, exciting the imagination and honing critical facilities. But lectures work less well with visual learners than auditory learners, so I would hope that anyone doing a lecture applies the Seeing, Hearing and Doing principle and has plenty of visual aids and perhaps offers the opportunity for moving around, rearranging or re-ordering sticky notes, and so on! Also, lectures will not help you to demonstrate your understanding – an important stage of the cycle. And learners need time to reflect not just on what they have learned but also on how they have learned it!

Q

But surely there is a 'best way' to teach?

A

We have long known that variety is the spice of life but now we have a theory showing us why and how different activities appeal to different learners and can be used for different purposes. It is not variety for the sake of variety but specific activities targeted for a purpose. The beauty of the cycle is that it focuses us on how people learn and this moves us beyond 'either/or' teaching methods, such as individual versus group-based, lecture-based versus inquiry-based. There is no universal best teaching practice. We need to select from a variety, a repertoire of teaching strategies with a particular purpose in mind. For example, we know that we are social animals and that most 'natural' learning does not just happen on its own but through working with someone else (for example, apprenticeship) or learning from a larger group, as we do in a family. It would be important, therefore, to build this understanding into our range of teaching strategies. In fact, for the interpersonal learner that is how they learn best. We may select a variety of teaching strategies to appeal to all different types of learners within the same lesson, say through a carousel of activities in the Activation stage of the cycle, or it may be that we only do one particular type of activity appealing to say the visual learner but next time we see the group we do a mainly kinesthetic activity. The key idea here is that it is planned and sequential, a conscious choice of activity with a purpose in mind based on a knowledge of the different learning styles in our classroom.

Q

How long should a cycle take?

A

Ideally within a single lesson (55 or 60 minutes minimum) you would go through all the stages in the cycle; however, some departments prefer to use a double lesson per cycle. In some cases you go through the cycle over a longer period but all the while you remind the students of the stages 'we have gone through' and the stages to come.

Q

We have a particular problem in this school with boys' achievement. Will this help?

A

Here is a list of some 'boy friendly' practices:

Devise clearly structured lessons, connected to their learning with outcomes made clear.

Evaluate the gender bias of resources and topics for study.

Enhance self-esteem through rewards and display of work.

Allow movement with a purpose: tell the class why this will help them to learn.

Learn by 'trying out' rather than being told about – investigative learning.

Build on boys' spatial awareness – give them success with plans and maps – teach them to use mind maps.

Build up a collection of objects for students to touch.

Act out stories, events and concepts.

Allow for competition.

Use ICT as part of teaching and learning.

Put the learning in context – why are we learning this? Show the Big Picture.

Break the learning into chunks.

Develop peer tutoring systems – including paired writing.

Introduce shared reading – pair competent boy readers with those of low self-esteem.

Monitor teacher talk – there is evidence to suggest that, although teachers believe they treat boys and girls the same, it rarely seems to be the case.

Make references to appropriate role models – Steven Biddulph, an Australian behavioural psychologist specializing in bringing up boys, says that children are 'role-seeking missiles'.

Have high expectations – build in challenge to engage and enhance performance and set stepped, achievable targets.

Talk to the boys themselves to discover their expectations and aspirations, their fears and concerns, and support and encourage them every step of the way.

Notice how well these practices relate to Accelerated Learning techniques!

Q

How do I find time to prepare these lessons?

A

You prepare lessons anyway. Right? Like all teachers you want your students to enjoy their lessons, be involved and make progress. The Accelerated Learning Cycle provides a successful framework to achieve this outcome. At first it will take time but as you use the framework and the tips in this book, you will find it becomes second nature. A good analogy is learning how to drive. It took time at first and conscious effort but now it is almost automatic.

You may also wish to try reducing marking and spending the saved time on preparation. See smart marking section on pages 58–63 for ideas. Get others involved so you can swap ideas and lessons. At first take it slowly. Try one lesson per week and work up to one per day. Take it at your own pace. Enjoy seeing your creativity come to life!

Q

Does it work with all students, even the disaffected?

A

There is always a temptation to give difficult students 'busy work' – copying, making notes, drawing diagrams – to keep them occupied. This is nothing to do with learning, it is to do with control and in the long run will lead to more disaffection because the learners are not engaged with the work. Good Accelerated Learning is motivating for students and will make disaffection less of an issue.

Well-focused teaching goes a long way in meeting the needs of students of all abilities, including the gifted and talented and those with special educational needs. Accelerated Learning is really for all and is often appreciated the most by the disaffected because it pays close attention to the individual learner – their preconceptions, learning styles, self-esteem and progress. As such it better meets the needs of those learners most disaffected by so-called traditional methods that concentrate on the needs of the class rather than the individual. It acknowledges particularly the needs of the kinesthetic learner – those who like to learn by doing.

Introducing Accelerated Learning into your school

'We see, we feel, we change.'

In introducing any significant change – and changing the way people teach is pretty significant – there are a number of golden rules:

1 All change is emotionally charged. You are asking people to make a leap of faith. They need to see, feel and experience the change in order to accept it and make sense of it.

2 Change needs to be top down and bottom up. Heads and heads of department have power and access to resources. They need to be worked with and on. Ignore them at your peril. People will resist top down only change. Some of the 'indians' need to be involved and enthusiastic as well as the 'chiefs'!

3 Think big but start small – in a year group or department, and so on. Then use success to breed success and bring more on board.

4 It is not how you see it that's important, it is how others see it. Constantly check that they understand what is needed. Address their anxieties, provide resources, training and, above all, time for preparation and reflection.

5 Change goes through different stages. All are important and need careful consideration. All have traps best avoided!

Stage 1

Getting others to see the need for change

People are less likely to change what they do because they are given analysis that shifts their thinking than because they are shown a truth that influences their feelings. In other words, it is an emotional response and this should not come as a surprise to an Accelerated Learning teacher! Teachers will tend to think that such and such methods worked for me in the past, so how do we help colleagues to see a different and better future?

stage 1

The classic mistake is to present too complex a picture – almost a 'laundry list' of why we should change. In this case what often happens is that people zero into the not so important contrasts rather than the critical ones. The way around this is to adopt the KISS principle, which stands for Keep It Simple Stupid!

1 Focus on what you think are the core contrasts between the present and what Accelerated Learning will do in the future. Do not dilute with too much complexity! For example, key advantages might be:

a) Students will be more involved and engaged in their learning.

b) You will know if the students really understand what they have learned.

c) Accelerated Learning caters for the different learning styles of our students.

d) The cycle puts good practice in the right order.

2 Make sure that the experience involves as many of the senses as possible. In particular, seeing the change in action makes for a memorable experience. Effective therefore would be:

a) Videos of Accelerated Learning in action together with student responses.

b) Visiting a school that is using Accelerated Learning techniques. There is nothing like seeing a real school with real students in action and talking to the staff and students about the experience.

c) Survey the students for their present views on their learning experience. How would they like it improved?

What is clear is that you cannot bulldoze change. It needs both top down and bottom up strategies to successfully implement educational change. According to Professor Michael Fullen, an international authority on change, top down strategies alone bring grief but no relief and bottom up strategies alone bring the odd spurt that eventually becomes inert!

In trying to persuade people of the need to introduce Accelerated Learning, remember the iceberg principle and show only the tip of the argument, keeping the rest in reserve. Perhaps use no more that three or four key points but remember that saying them once will not be enough. The key points may well have to be re-visited half a dozen times before colleagues really come to accept the argument.

Remember too the need to bring on board key players who wield power and influence (heads, heads of department). It is very difficult to work around them, so involve them in identifying the problem and help them to come to your solution!

Two tools useful for starting the debate on the need for change are the Sigmoid curve and a simple compare and contrast matrix of 'natural learning' versus 'secondary school learning'. These are effective because both are visual and both can be related to people on a personal (emotional) level. The Sigmoid curve, for example, can also be used to chart the rise and (eventual) fall of the local football team (do you bring in young players when the team is doing well or when things are on the decline) and the problems of Marks & Spencer and the demise of C&A. Moving jobs when you are happy and successful seems to be good advice when contrasted with the desperation often felt of 'trying to get out'. The important point here is that change is often best when things are going well, since if you do not change, the odds are things will get worse and then change will be very much harder. This is useful stuff to use with good or complacent departments or schools.

The Sigmoid curve

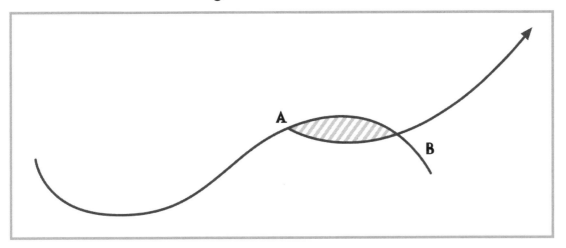

Handy (1994) suggests that most organizations rise and fall or expand and contract in a way very similar to a sine wave. The challenge for leadership in successful schools/departments is to spot when the organization is at point A and to re-engineer so that the school/department does not rest on its laurels when it is still improving. It must take the risk of moving on to a new Sigmoid curve and not wait to change until it is moving downwards at point B. Handy expresses this as follows:

'The right place to start that second curve is at point A, where there is time, as well as the resources and the energy, to get the curve through its initial explorations and floundering before the first curve begins to dip downwards. That would seem obvious; were it not for the fact that at point A all the messages coming through to the individual or the institution are that everything is going fine, that it would be folly to change when the current recipes are working so well. All that we know of change, be it personal change or change in organizations, tells us that the real energy for change only comes when you are looking disaster in the face, at point B on the first curve. At this point, however, it is going to require a mighty effort to drag oneself up to where, by now, one should be on the second curve.'
(Handy 1994, pages 51-52)

Natural learning versus secondary learning

Also resonating with personal experience, whether as a parent, teacher or child, is the natural learning versus secondary school learning chart. If, as seems reasonable, we are all hard-wired to learn, then little of 'natural learning' survives to transfer to secondary education. Accelerated Learning can help to correct this balance!

Natural Learning	Secondary Learning
concrete experience images	abstract concepts
holographic processing	words
learning by doing and mimicry	linear processing
learning in context	learning by reading
learning with others	learning out of context
	learning by yourself

Stage 2

We see the need to change but fail to move!

As we get nearer to a significant change we tend to get more anxious about it. If we fail to address people's natural anxieties and concerns, we will get what is known as the 'implementation dip' where things do not start at all well. Most of us do not like the thought of doing something new poorly, especially if we are already good at something else. We should not underestimate – what is often initially well concealed – the fear of looking stupid or incompetent.

An old joke goes something like this. On a dark night a man has lost his ring and a passer-by sees him searching and pauses to ask 'What did you lose?' 'My ring' comes the reply. The conversation continues 'Where did you lose it?' 'Way over there' the desperate searcher answers. 'Then why are you looking here?' queries the passer-by. 'Because this is where the light is' replies the hopeless searcher.

In schools, we often stay where the light is, even when we recognize that it is the wrong place. Similarly, we often stick to what we are good at even when we see it has become irrelevant.

So what do you do?

1 Address directly anxieties and concerns. Listen carefully to what people have to say. They may see something that you in your zeal have overlooked.

ACCELERATED LEARNING – A User's Guide

2 Remove any obstacles:

a) Lack of time

Provide time for teachers to plan and review together by rearranging the school week to finish early on one day. Divide meetings into operational and strategic. The urgent often drives out the important, so safeguard your strategic time for planning and review.

b) Lack of expertise

Appoint 'learning coaches' who work with teachers in the classrooms. Two in the classroom can help overcome discipline fears. Provide INSET and visits to other schools.

c) Feeling overwhelmed

Think big but start small giving colleagues time to get used to the innovation. Choose a year group/department/class to start off Accelerated Learning. Then build on the success.

A classic mistake at this stage is that since you see the need for change you assume that everyone else does. It is at this stage that you need to check for understanding. How clearly do your colleagues see where they are going? Ask them to describe each key element of the Accelerated Learning Cycle. Then ask them what it will require from them in terms of personal capabilities. One school used a scenario challenge to check whether their staff had a clear understanding of Accelerated Learning. This is often a good and safe way for concerns and anxieties to be addressed.

Scenario challenge

Essential question
In what way does Accelerated Learning provide a framework for effective teaching and learning?

Challenge
You must present the case for Accelerated Learning to an audience of teachers, organized into groups of four or five, at a school where you have just been employed. The aim of your presentation will be to convince them that they should take this framework on board as a means of developing teaching and learning in their school/department. This is the first time your audience will have heard of the model. Although the audience are not cynical, they may well be critical and ask questions such as:

'Won't students get sick of the same kind of lessons all the time?'
'How can I sustain this kind of teaching?'
'How does this model encourage collaborative learning?'
'Will I be able to cover the syllabus content in time?'
'Is Accelerated Learning suitable for the most able and least able?'

Product criteria
Your presentation should last for a maximum of ten minutes and include:

an explanation of the principles underpinning Accelerated Learning.

- practical examples of classroom practice.
- an attempt to answer the above questions.
- a graphic or visual image or diagram that can be seen by your audience and that each group can talk about.
- a memorable quote or saying or slogan that 'hooks' your audience and forms part of your graphic/visual image.
- a simple paragraph containing no more that three sentences summarizing why you think this approach can make learning much more interesting and effective.

NB All members of each group should take part in the presentation. Finally, have fun and remember that the most memorable presentations are humorous in some way.

Stage 3

You can start to lose momentum

People get tired! Change requires energy and effort. There is a danger that things can drift and the momentum is not sustained. At this stage there is a need for:

1 Champions! Colleagues close to the action encouraging and supporting. Perhaps working alongside colleagues in their classroom as a 'learning coach' using techniques like 'you plan and I'll teach to your plan' and then reversing it 'I'll plan and you teach'.

2 Celebrating 'wins'. Sharing successes and making much of the students' reactions. A video of a successful lesson or an interview with the students where they identify what has changed and how they like the new approach. The more the outcomes of change are visible, measurable and unambiguous the better.

3 Look for ways to reward colleagues for their efforts; for example, allocate them a laptop, share successful lesson plans thereby saving individual planning and time. Cramlington Community High School rewards staff every time they are observed teaching using Accelerated Learning with a £75 credit that can be used towards staff development. Colleagues can accumulate their credits and the school will match pound for pound when they wish to 'cash' them in. This way colleagues can finance INSET abroad or purchase for exclusive school use a digital camera or VCR.

Stage 4

Embedding the change so it becomes part of the whole culture

It is important to pay particular attention to recruitment and induction of new staff. By being clear in what you are looking for you are more likely to get a 'match' so that new colleagues joining the school or department are in tune with the culture for Accelerated Learning. The recruitment process could involve interviewees planning a lesson using the Accelerated Learning

stage 4

Cycle and the induction process might consist of a full day's training. Within the school new initiatives need to be aligned to Accelerated Learning. The lesson observation pro forma used for Performance Management can, for example, be designed to keep good teaching and learning at the forefront of everyone's thoughts. Similarly, ICT should support Accelerated Learning. Here is a valuable peg on which to hang the ICT hat!

The school or departmental development plan should also be firmly rooted in priorities for successful teaching and learning. Accelerated Learning should be at the heart of the school or department – this needs to be reflected in the documentation that the school or department produces. And, of course, if you are really clever, you can model the cycle in your departmental and staff meetings and INSET days. Other ways to keep Accelerated Learning at the forefront of all colleagues' minds can include:

 buying colleagues a teacher planner where the introductory pages are customized and include 'handy hints' on Accelerated Learning.

 publishing for colleagues a 'Teaching for Learning Bulletin'. If it is useful, practical, stimulating and readable it will keep teaching and learning visible and upfront.

 inviting colleagues from other schools to observe lessons. There is nothing like the approval of your peers to build confidence and make you feel you are really doing something worthwhile. It also keeps you on your toes!

It is important to ensure that what you think is going on is actually going on! Formal monitoring of classrooms is one way to do this, as is an informal 'walk through' – stopping to talk to teachers and looking at students' work and the learning in which they are engaged.

Finally, regular surveys of the students' views through questionnaires provide invaluable data. Publish the results.

The classic mistake at this stage is to think you have the change cracked and move on to something else. Preaching to the converted, far from being a superfluous activity, is vital. Preachers do it every Sunday! The strengthening of the commitment and the morale of those on board is an essential task in order to both bind them more closely and make them more effective exponents of Accelerated Learning.

'Change is a journey not a blueprint.'
Michael Fullan

You never quite know if you have arrived at your destination until people start saying 'Accelerated Learning? – Well, it's just the way we do things around here.'

section **FIVE**

Accelerated **L**earning
– resources

In Section Five you will find details of

references

recommended reading

useful websites

questionnaire

pro formas

references
reading
websites
questionnaire
pro formas

References

Amis, Kingsley (1980) *Jake's Thing*, London: Penguin

Assessment Reform Group (1999) *Assessment for Learning: Beyond the Black Box*, London: Kings College

Black, P. and Wiliam, D. (1998) *Inside the Black Box*, London: King's College

Bloom, B. (1956) *The Taxonomy of Educational Objectives*, London: Longman

Clarke, Shirley (2001) *Unlocking Formative Assessment*, London: Hodder & Stoughton Educational

Dunn, Rita and Dunn, Kenneth (1978) *Teaching Students Through Their Individual Learning Styles*, Englewood Cliffs, NJ: Prentice-Hall

Gardner, Howard (1993) *Multiple Intelligences: The Theory in Practice*, New York: Basic Books

Grinder, M. (1991) *Righting the Educational Conveyor Belt*, Portland, OR: Metamorphous Press

Handy, Charles (1994) *The Empty Raincoat*, London: Hutchinson Extract reproduced with permission from The Random House Group Ltd.

Hattie, J.A. (1992) *'Measuring the effects of schooling'*, Australian Journal of Education 36(1), 5–13

Hermann, Ned (1997) *The Hermann Brain Dominance Instrument*, Lake Lure, NC: Hermann International

Hughes, Mike (1999) *Closing the Learning Gap*, Stafford: Network Educational Press

Hyerle, David (2000) *A Field Guide to using Visual Tools*, Alexandria, VA: ASCD Publishing

Marzano, R. (2001) *What Works in Schools*, Alexandria, VA: ASCD Publishing

Rose, C. and Nicholl, M.J. (1997) *Accelerated Learning for the 21st Century*, New York: Delacorte Press

Sapolsky, R. (1998) *Why Zebras don't get Ulcers: An Updated Guide to Stress, Stress Related Diseases, and Coping*, New York: Freeman

Sills, Beverley (2003) quoted in Paul Arden, *It's Not How Good you Are, It's How Good You Want to Be*, London: Phaidon

Vygotsky, L.S. (1978) *Mind in Society*, Cambridge, MA: Harvard University Press

Recommended reading

section **FIVE**

A selection of books by the authors

Smith, Alistair *(1998)* ***Accelerated Learning in Practice****, Stafford: Network Educational Press*

Smith, Alistair *(2002)* ***The Brain's Behind It****, Stafford: Network Educational Press*

Smith, Alistair and Call, Nicola *(1999)* ***The ALPS Approach: Accelerated Learning in Primary Schools****, Stafford: Network Educational Press*

Smith, Alistair and Call, Nicola *(2001)* ***The ALPS Approach Resource Book****, Stafford: Network Educational Press*

Smith, Alistair and Lucas, Bill *(2002)* ***Help Your Child to Succeed****, Stafford: Network Educational Press*

Smith, Alistair and Lyseight-Jones, Pauline *(2003)* ***Moving On: A Quality Framework for Accelerated Learning****, Alite Ltd*

Wise, Derek and Lovatt, Mark *(2001)* ***Creating an Accelerated Learning School****, Stafford: Network Educational Press*

20 books for your school library

Bransford, Brown and Cocking *(1999)* ***How People Learn: Brain, Mind, Experience and School****, US National Research Council*
300-plus pages of quality insights

Call, N. and Featherstone, S. *(2002)* ***The Thinking Child****,*
Stafford: Network Educational Press
Brain-based learning for the foundation stage

Carter, R. *(1998)* ***Mapping the Mind****, London: Wiedenfeld & Nicolson*
Best summary to date for the lay reader

Caviglioli, O. and Harris, I. *(2001)* ***MapWise****, Stafford: Network Educational Press*
Moves beyond mind mapping; looks terrific

Claxton, Guy *(2003)* ***Building Learner Power****, Bristol: TLO*
The author's case for a more holistic view of life-long learning

Costa, A. *(ed.) (2001)* ***Developing Minds: A Resource Book for Teaching Thinking****, Alexandria, VA: ASCD Publishing*
A collection of articles for those who teach thinking

Gilbert, Ian *(2002)* ***Essential Motivation****, London: Routledge*
Easily accessible thoughts about motivation in the classroom

Ginnis, Paul *(2002)* ***The Teacher's Toolkit****, Bancyfelin, Carmarthen: Crown House*
Carefully written and thoroughly researched, linking theory to practice

Goleman, Daniel *(1996)* ***Emotional Intelligence – Why it Matters More than IQ****, London: Bloomsbury*
The book that launched the movement

Goleman, Boyatzis and McKee *(2002)* ***Primal Leadership****, Cambridge, MA: Harvard Business School Press*
Give it to your headteacher

Gopnik, A., Meltzoff, A. and Kuhl, P. *(1999)* ***How Babies Think,*** *London: Wiedenfeld & Nicolson*
Blows a small hole in Piaget's boat!

Greany, Toby and Rodd, Jill *(2003)* ***Creating a Learning to Learn School****, (Campaign for Learning), Stafford: Network Educational Press*
Useful resource that emerged from the Learning to Learn project

Howard, Pierce J. *(2000)* ***The Owner's Manual for the Brain****, 2nd edn, Texas: Bard Press*
Comprehensive and very readable overview of the psychology and physiology of learning

Mahoney, Terry *(2003)* ***Words Work: How to Change Your Language to Improve Behaviour in the Classroom****, Bancyfelin, Carmarthen: Crown House*
NLP in schools

Novak, John *(2002)* ***Inviting Educational Leadership****, Harlow: Pearson Education*
And why not invite educational leadership to read it?

Perkins, D. *(1992)* ***Smart Schools****, New York: Free Press*
Harvard professor's view on thinking schools

Rockett, M. and Percival, S. *(2002)* ***Thinking for Learning****, Stafford: Network Educational Press*
Good overview of different practical approaches to teaching thinking skills

Rupp, Rebecca *(1998)* ***Committed to Memory****, New York: Crown*
Concise overview of memory techniques

Senge, Peter *(2000)* ***Schools That Learn****, London: Nicholas Brealey*
Fifth discipline field book for educators

Vos, J. and Dryden, G. *(2001)* ***The Learning Revolution****, Stafford: Network Educational Press*
An overview of some world trends in learning

Useful websites

Authors

www.alite.co.uk	*Alistair Smith*
www.cchs.northumbria.sch.uk	*Derek Wise and Mark Lovatt*

Learning environments

www.edunova.co.uk	*Learning Environments Company*
www.bottledwater.org.	*International Bottled Water Association*
www.british-sleep-society.org.uk/	*British Sleep Society*
www.braingym.org	*Dennison's Brain Gym® organization*
www.lboro.ac.uk/departments/hu/groups/sleep/	*Sleep research laboratory, Loughborough*

Learning styles

www.gregorc.com	*Anthony Gregorc*
www.mind-map.com	*Tony Buzan*
www.thomasarmstrong.com	*Thomas Armstrong*
www.ltip.psychology.org	*Learning theory synopsis*
www.universaleducator.com/LearnStyle/index.html	*Excellent starting point for learning styles research*
www.advisorteam.com/user/ktsintro.asp	*Kiersey Temperament Sorter*
www.knowyourtype.com	*Myers-Briggs Type Indicator*

Learning of the future

www.itaa.org	*Information Technology Association of America*
www.pzweb.harvard.edu/Research/Research	*The official Harvard Project Zero site*
www.vtc.ngfl.gov.uk	*Virtual Teacher Centre*
www.epic.co.uk	*Leading thinking in e-learning*
www.nestafuturelab.org	*New modes of learning*
www.rsa.org.uk/newcurriculum	*Opening Minds Project*

www.allianceforchildhood.net/	*Alliance for Childhood*
www.cdi.page.com	*The Child Development Institute*

Organizations

www.ialearn.org	*International Alliance for Learning*
www.campaign-for-learning.org.uk	*Campaign for Learning*
www.21learn.org	*21st Century Learning Initiative*
www.transformingschools.org.uk	*Portal promising access to over 500 education sites*
www.ufa.org.uk	*University of the First Age*
www.buildinglearningpower.co.uk	*A more holistic view of learning*
www.hse.org.uk	*Human Scale Education*
www.ascd.org	*US professional membership organization for school managers*
www.clcrc.com	*The Co-operative Learning Centre*
www.seal.org.uk	*Society for Effective Affective Learning*

Thinking skills approaches

www.sapere.net	*Advancement of Philosophical Enquiry and Reflection in Education*
www.p4c.net	*Philosophy for Children*
www.modellearning.com	*Mapping techniques*
www.case-network.org	*Cognitive acceleration*
www.thethinkingclassroom.co.uk	*Thinking classrooms in practice*
www.psych.qub.ac.uk/staff/mcguinness.html	*Carol McGuiness and her work*
www.teachingthinking.net	*Robert Fisher's website*
www.kcl.ac.uk/depsta/education/teaching/CASE.html	*CASE website*
www.edwdebono.com	*Edward de Bono site*
www.thinkingcap.org.uk	*Philosophy for children website*
www.dialogueworks.co.uk	*Philosophy for children website*

Learning and motivation

www.eiconsortium.org/members/goleman.htm	*Emotional Intelligence*
www.nelig.com	*National emotional literacy site*
www.antidote.org.uk	*UK campaign for emotional literacy*
www.kcl.ac.uk/depsta/education/publications/blackbox.html	
	Inside the Black Box
www.learningfirst.org	*Learning First Alliance*
www.casel.org	*Social and emotional learning*
www.education.man.ac.uk/cfas.htm	*Centre for Formative Assessment Studies*
www.stanford.edu/group/CRE/motivation.html	*Motivation research*
www.reviewing.co.uk/index.html	*Facilitating active learning*
www.haygroup.com	*Hay Group on teacher effectiveness*

The official view

www.ncsl.org.uk	*National College for School Leadership (UK)*
www.teachernet.gov.uk/bprs	*Best practice research scholarships*
www.ngfl.gov.uk	*National Grid for Learning*
www.qca.org.uk	*Qualifications and Curriculum Agency*
www.canteach.gov.uk	*Teacher Training Agency*
www.scre.ac.uk	*Scottish Council for Research into Education*

Some training and development organizations

www.thesolutionsfocus.com	*Practical problem solving for everyday challenges*
www.brainconnection.com	*Brain connection site*
www.brain.com	*Brain.com site*
www.6seconds.org/	*Emotional Intelligence organization*
www.newhorizons.org	*Publishers of brain-based materials*
www.21learn.org	*The 21st Century Learning Initiative*
www.aptt.com/	*Edward De Bono training organization*
www.scilearn.com	*Scientific Learning Corporation*

Learning difference

www.ldresources.com	*Learning Disabilities Resources is a US online resource site*
www.ldonline.org	*Overview of Learning Disabilities*
www.pavilion.co.uk/add/english.html	*ADD links*
www.bda-dyslexia.org.uk/	*British Dyslexia Association*
www.emmbrook.demon.co.uk/dysprax/homepage.htm	
	The Dyspraxia Foundation
www.nagcbritain.org.uk	*National Association for Gifted Children*
www.edwebproject.org/edref.mi.intro.html	*Multiple Intelligences site*

Learning and brain research

www.brainresearch.com	*Recommended for comprehensive links*
www.jlcbrain.com	*Eric Jensen*
www.loloville.com/brain_based_learning.htm	*Good starting point for brain-based learning*
www.cainelearning.com	*Geoffrey and Renate Caine*
www.bps.org.uk/	*British Psychological Society*
www.apa.org	*American Psychological Association*
www.brainland.com	*Neuroscience information*
www.med.harvard.edu/AANLIB/	*The Whole Brain Atlas*
www.science.ca/scientists/Kimura/kimura.html	*Gender and brain organization*
www.ion.ucl.ac.uk/	*University College London Institute of Neurology*
www.uci.edu/	*University of California at Irvine*

Music and learning

www.mozartcenter.com/index.html
www.musica.uci.edu/

www.mindinst.org/

www.mri.ac.uk/index.html
www.srpmme.u-net.com/

Tomatis method
MuSICA Music and Science
Information Computer Archive
MIND Institute Research into the
Mozart Effect and Education
UK-based music research centre
Society for Research in Psychology of
Music and Music Education

Questionnaire

Use this questionnaire to reflect on your own practice

	USUALLY	SOMETIMES	NEEDS ATTENTION
I apply recent knowledge about learning to plan effective lessons			
I change the furniture in my lessons to facilitate the learning activity			
My classroom has attractive displays including students' work			
I use my classroom display as a teaching aid			
I make my students feel welcome when they arrive in the classroom			
I pre-warn my students that I am going to ask them questions			
I don't allow my students to put each other down			
I don't use 'put downs' or sarcasm in my classroom			
I establish clear learning outcomes and display them somewhere prominently in my classroom			
I refer to the learning outcomes throughout the lesson and especially as part of the review			
I connect the lesson to what has gone before			
I provide clear signposts for the learning journey: the Big Picture			
I make it clear to my students why they should 'buy in' to learning the topic			
When I present lessons/material I use visual stimulus			
I give my students the opportunity to exchange views and opinions			
I don't answer my own questions!			

	USUALLY	SOMETIMES	NEEDS ATTENTION
I allow time for my students to think when asked questions			
I give my students the opportunity for physical movement in my lesson			
I use feedback throughout the lesson			
I plan my lessons in the knowledge that students learn in different ways			
I use collaborative (co-operative) learning techniques			
I allow time for students to work independently			
I have whole-class discussions			
I try to engage my students' emotions through use of evocative music, film, prose or poetry			
I use games or activities that involve my students in the lesson			
I use colour in a purposeful way in my lessons			
I ensure my students have the opportunity to demonstrate their new understanding			
I review the key learning points in my lessons			
I try and tease out with my students how they have learned			

Pro Formas

This section provides practical resources for teachers. Feel free to photocopy these pro formas. Blow them up to A3 and use to plan lessons in the Accelerated Learning Cycle or adapt and change as you see fit.

Topic: .... Lesson: .... Date: ....

CONNECT

ACTIVATE

DEMONSTRATE

CONSOLIDATE

PRO FORMAS

Subject	Monday	Tuesday	Wednesday	Thursday	Friday	
CONNECT **Use input/activity to agree:** 1 What we already know and what would be useful to know (content). 2 How we will learn (process). 3 How today's learning fits into the whole topic (benefits).						**Resources**
ACTIVATE **Pose problems and present new information through different channels.** Visual Auditory Kinesthetic Other						
DEMO **Structure activities around the problems posed.** Activity Feedback and review Activity Feedback and review						**Assessment**
CONS. **Agree:** What has been learned? How have we learned? How can we use our learning?						

Date ----------

Topic _____   Lesson _____   Date _____

CONNECT

Use input/activity to agree:
1 What we already know and what would be useful to know (content).
2 How we will learn (process).
3 How today's learning fits into the whole topic (benefits).

ACTIVATE

Pose problems and present new information through different channels.
Visual
Auditory
Kinesthetic
Other

DEMO

Structure activities around the problems posed.
Activity
Feedback and review
Activity
Feedback and review

CONS.

Agree:
What has been learned?
How have we learned?
How can we use our learning?

Resources

Assessment

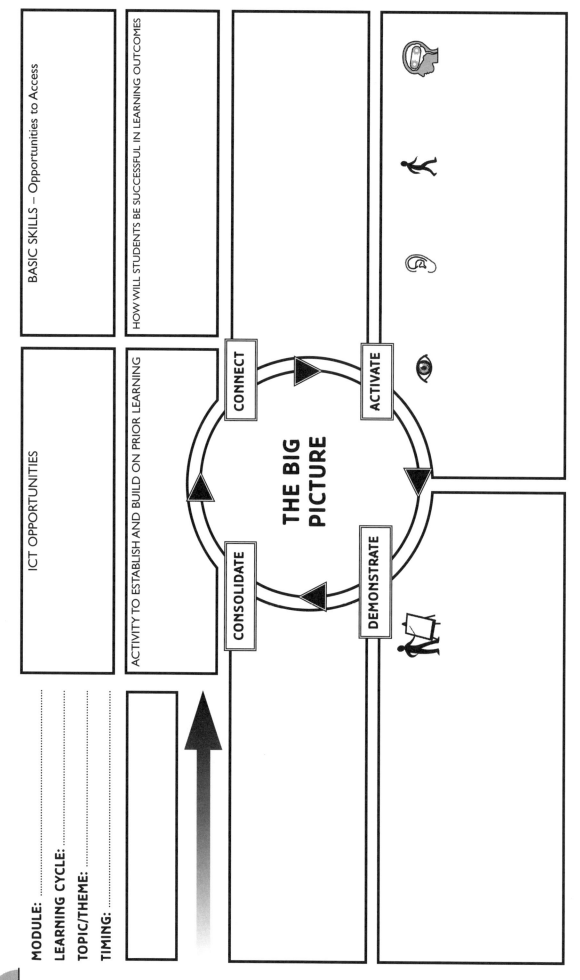

MODULE: ....

LEARNING CYCLE: ....

TOPIC/THEME: ....

TIMING: ....

ICT OPPORTUNITIES

BASIC SKILLS – Opportunities to Access

ACTIVITY TO ESTABLISH AND BUILD ON PRIOR LEARNING

HOW WILL STUDENTS BE SUCCESSFUL IN LEARNING OUTCOMES

CONNECT

ACTIVATE

CONSOLIDATE

DEMONSTRATE

THE BIG PICTURE

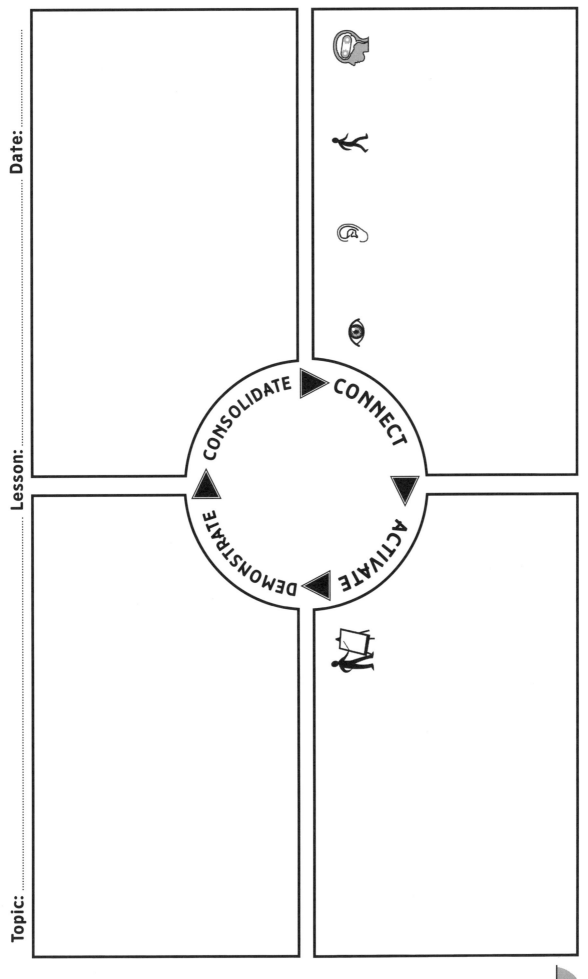

Date:

Lesson:

Topic:

Lesson		Date		Resources
CONNECT				
ACTIVATE				
DEMONSTRATE				Assessment
CONSOLIDATE				

ACCELERATED LEARNING – A User's Guide

Index

M

N

O

P

Q

R

S

T

V

W

INDEX